Choosing Small

The Essential Guide to Successful High School Conversion

Jay Feldman, M. Lisette López, and Katherine G. Simon

Foreword by Michael Klonsky

JOSSEY-BASS
A Wiley Imprint
www.josseybass.com

Published by Jossey-Bass
A Wiley Imprint
989 Market Street, San Francisco, CA 94103-1741   www.josseybass.com

Jossey-Bass books and products are available through most bookstores. To contact Jossey-Bass directly
call our Customer Care Department within the U.S. at 800-956-7739, outside the U.S. at 317-572-3986,
or fax 317-572-4002.

Jossey-Bass also publishes its books in a variety of electronic formats. Some content that appears in print
may not be available in electronic books.

Library of Congress Cataloging-in-Publication Data

Feldman, Jay, date.
   Choosing small the essential guide to successful high school conversion / Jay Feldman,
M. Lisette López, and Katherine G. Simon; foreword by Michael Klonsky.
      p. cm.—(The Jossey-Bass education series)
   Includes bibliographical references and index.
   ISBN-13: 978–0–7879–8027–6 (alk. paper)
   ISBN-10: 0–7879–8027–7 (alk. paper)
      1. High schools—United States. 2. School size—United States. 3. School autonomy—United States.
   4. School improvement programs—United States. I. López, M. Lisette. II. Simon, Katherine G., date.
   III. Title. IV. Series.
   LB1620.F42 2006
   373.12—dc22   2005021211

Printed in the United States of America
FIRST EDITION
PB Printing   10 9 8 7 6 5 4 3 2 1

The Jossey-Bass Education Series

Contents

Foreword — vii

Preface — xi

Acknowledgments — xv

The Coalition of Essential Schools — xvii

The Authors — xix

PART ONE   TOWARD A COMMON PURPOSE

1. Education for the Information Age — 3

2. Leading the Process — 14

3. The District: Supporting Change and Working with Autonomies — 37

4. Stakeholder Engagement — 55

PART TWO   FOUNDING AUTONOMOUS, INTERCONNECTED SCHOOLS

5. School Vision — 71

6. Transforming Instructional Practice — 82

7. Essentials of Small School Leadership — 91

8. Handling Electives, AP Classes, and Other Access Issues — 102

9. Sharing the Building — 110

PART THREE   TRANSITION PLANNING

10. Roll-Out Plans for New Autonomous Small Schools — 121

11. Student Choice Options — 135

12. Teacher Assignment and Contractual Issues — 143

13. Concluding Thoughts — 154

Appendix A: Profiled Organizations   157

Appendix B: Profiled Schools   161

Appendix C: Additional School Design Resources   166

Appendix D: Model Guidelines for Small Schools   180

Appendix E: Plans, Processes, and Policies for a   184
Conversion Strategy

Appendix F: The Harwood Institute's Principles   190
of Civic Engagement

References   193

Index   199

Foreword

In the world of school research, the issue of school size has basically been resolved, at least for now. Advocates of small schools and *smaller learning communities* would have a difficult time finding worthy opponents in the research world these days. As one feisty university small school researcher told me recently: "It's getting downright boring. There's nobody left to argue with." We have come a long way since the late 1950s when, in the wake of the Soviet Union's *Sputnik* launch, the Carnegie Institute's James Bryant Conant published his study *The American High School Today,* lauding the potential benefits of the large comprehensive high school, not only as a means to winning the arms race with the Russians but as a tool for democ-ratizing our own society and finding tracks to college or gainful employ-ment for students from varying backgrounds. While we may have won the race to put arms in outer space, the large comprehensive high schools that are Conant's legacy have for the most part become factories of failure for more than half of their population.

The case for restructuring these factories has now been made, and it is a compelling one. *Choosing Small: The Essential Guide to Successful High School Conversion* makes the case even stronger and adds a new frame of reference—high school conversion, or turning large high schools into small ones that use the same buildings.

When it comes to improving learning outcomes for kids, especially for children of color and those from low-income families, smaller is better, safer, and more likely to narrow the so-called achievement gap. The problem is that educational research often has minimal impact when it comes to the design, structure, and culture of schools.

As a nation, we will spend more than half a trillion dollars on school construction over the next decade—and most of that money will go into building bigger and bigger schools despite the abundance of evidence to the contrary. The planning, policies, and resource allocations for this new school construction will not be driven so much by educational research as by political priorities, real estate interests, financial constraints, and perceived economies of scale. It is not unusual in cities like New York, Chicago, Miami, and Los Angeles to see schools of three thousand to five thousand students. The reader will probably not be surprised to learn that the high school completion rates in those cities and within those large schools are among the lowest in the nation. Only after these fortresses have been built does the occasional board member or superintendent ask: "What are we going to do inside this building and will the design meet the educational plan?"

The past decade has seen the discussion among school reformers move beyond the small-large debate to one of *how?* What's the strategy for systemic change? How do we organize as a community to transform our large, often low-performing traditional high schools into places where kids are visible and where teachers work together in family- or community-type environs? How can we engage parents and community residents to see beyond their own traditional high school experience to dream of new possibilities for their children? How do we move policymakers, funders, school boards, and school district administrators to support the birth and regeneration of new school models and designs and give them a reasonable chance to grow and flourish? Even more important, how do we keep these new, smaller, redesigned schools and learning communities from simply becoming smaller versions of the large traditional schools, replete with the old inequities, top-down delivery systems of instruction, and cookie-cutter standardization? Finally, some question whether or not it is even possible to successfully transform our high schools and keep them as viable centers of public space? High school conversions like those highlighted in *Choosing Small* offer an alternative to privatization and the rule of the marketplace. While the road forward is difficult, the authors can offer enough examples of success to keep hope alive.

But there is little in the training or on-the-job experience of our whole educational establishment that has prepared anyone from the teacher corps through the district administration for this kind of structural and cultural transformation of the environment or for the necessary changes in everything from teaching methods through school governance. Fortunately help has come from a network of writers, researchers, fellow teachers, and outside supporters and funders. The small school movement has generated new models of collaboration and peer coaching, along with new strategies for high school redesign that range from autonomous new start-up schools through smaller learning communities within existing schools to groups of new autonomous schools that result from the conversion of a large traditional high school into multiple units sharing the same physical plant. Experience tells us that the latter is the most difficult but also the most necessary since that's where most of the kids are.

There are charter schools, pilot schools, multiplexes, contract schools, schools-within-a-school, career academies, advisories, and freshman centers. While the forms may differ, they all must share essential qualities and features described by the authors, like high degrees of personalization, organizational autonomy, and a strong sense of community.

This historic transformation (remember, high schools have remained unchanged for half a century or more) is being examined, documented, and given guidance in a new stream of books and articles. It is by some accounts the most studied reform ever, going back to the action research of the 1970s, with works such as Deborah Meier's *The Power of Their Ideas*, and to studies of urban school restructuring in cities like New York, Philadelphia, and Chicago by leading lights such as Michelle Fine and William Ayers.

Because the effort to convert large high schools is so much more than a technical or structural matter, the most helpful and insightful writings for me are those like *Choosing Small* that rely on the experiences, successful and not, of the practitioners, and on their own words, via interviews. Instead of pushing one top-down model of change or replication, the authors try and capture the essentials. And who better to do that than three writer-researchers like Jay Feldman, Lisette López, and Katherine Simon, who are based at the Coalition of Essential Schools. Coalition visionaries like Ted Sizer and Deborah Meier were among the original architects of the modern small school movement, and the Coalition's member schools have the greatest wealth of collective high school transformational experience for study and reflection.

The three authors each combine academic and research skills with active work experience in the small school movement. Simon helped to launch CES's current work to support the founding of new small schools and the conversion of comprehensive high schools into small schools. López, who has written extensively on issues of equity and diversity, has worked with youth programs and community agencies trying to meet the needs of diverse student populations. And Feldman worked for several years with the Center for Collaborative Education in Boston, doing research on the city's Pilot Schools and high school conversion efforts, and looking at external coaching, diversity, and parent involvement issues. The three authors know the research and know the movement.

If you are a teacher in a large comprehensive high school, trying to create a new learning environment for your kids and fellow teachers, you will find direction, hope, and strategies for success in *Choosing Small.* Parents, district leaders, principals, and policy groups will learn the lay of the land and be able to generate new ideas and plans after engaging with this work. The concepts are clear, the arguments for real transformation—not just tinkering—are strong, and the language is accessible.

Choosing Small is a good guide or road map for navigating a difficult but rewarding pathway.

—Michael Klonsky
Director, Small Schools Workshop
Chicago, Illinois

Preface

In the last five years, more and more districts across the country have opted to transform their large comprehensive high schools into new small schools. This book is based on in-depth conversations with school and community members involved in high school conversions. In it, we describe efforts to date, capturing the wisdom born in the experience of the pioneers of this work.

Many of the educators we interviewed asked us to emphasize that the work is hard. "Do not underestimate it," they warned. But they also wanted us to convey their passion for the task they have taken up. The people we spoke with embarked on the journey of school conversion because they wanted more for the young people they know. Some are motivated by a commitment to remedy inequities and to achieve social justice, by the urgency of contributing to a more fully participatory and democratic society, or by the desire that all children will develop their intellectual gifts. Some are motivated by the recognition that the demands of the new economy require a new kind of education. For these reasons and more, the consensus of the folks in the trenches—and often in the midst of yet-to-be-realized dreams—is that the difficult work of conversion is worth it.

Throughout our conversations, we heard a consistent refrain: Large high schools are not doing justice to our children. There is a better way. As Mary Anne Raywid writes, "We have confirmed [the positive effects of small schools] with a clarity and at a level of confidence rare in the annals of education research" (1999, p. 1). Although some educators believe that factory-model high schools were never well suited to children's needs and others believe that what we need from our schools has changed significantly in recent years, we heard a growing consensus that the country needs a new system of secondary education that prepares all children to participate in their world as thoughtful and productive citizens. These voices argue—and we concur—that we cannot merely tweak a system that is currently failing. We do not need reform. We need reinvention.

The reinvention envisioned by many on the forefront of the conversion effort requires more than creating smaller schools. It requires a cultural shift in the way that students, teachers, district staff, and community members view what schools do, what students need to know, how they learn, and how they can best be taught. Like any significant social change effort, such a paradigm shift requires giving up deeply internalized practices and ways of thinking, replacing them with a whole new set. The transformation of the actual large schools that stand behind the icon of the American High School requires deep shifts in instruction, school design, and school culture. The movement to create small schools, thus, is not about smallness in itself; it is a movement to create a different practice and vision of schooling—a vision in which all students are known well and are supported as they master significant intellectual challenges.

Based on our conversations with people who are leading school conversions, this book provides a framework for those doing conversion—from beginning to grapple with the idea of transforming a large school into small schools to crafting a design for each proposed new school, and from staging the opening of each school to having it fully emerge into its own identity. We report on what we see as the most promising practices for school conversion, recognizing that most of the conversions we report on are still very much works in progress. In this sense, we acknowledge that this book and the suggestions we make are also works in progress that will inevitably need revision as all of those involved in high school conversions—including, we hope, the readers of this book—carry the process forward and share their discoveries with the rest of us.

The Plan of This Book

This book is intended to help schools, districts, community groups, and educational organizations with the process of converting large comprehensive high schools into a system of small autonomous schools. In the next chapters, we share what we have learned about the complex nature of the conversion process and the depth of the transformation that occurs. This book is intended to be read as needed: chapters are organized around a common issue and we expect readers will want to read what they most need when they need it. We deal with the most challenging controversies that occur within conversion efforts:

- How does the change to multiple small autonomous high schools impact students' ability to choose a learning environment, their access to resources, and their preparation for college or career?

- How does the change to multiple small autonomous high schools impact teachers' working conditions—what they teach, where they teach, and even if they teach?

- Will special education students and English language learners receive the support they need to be successful?

- Is changing school size enough? Or is becoming a small learning community enough change? Are other changes (for example, granting autonomy over staffing and budget allocation) really necessary?

- To what degree do districts and schools restructure their relationship from centralized to decentralized, and how are schools supported to make the best use of new areas of local control?

- How do leaders of large schools find a new role and still allow for the independence of new schools and the growth of new leaders?

- How can school and community members come to a shared vision and understanding that all students are capable of achieving at college-ready levels and can be successful in postsecondary education?

- How can school and community members come to a shared vision and understanding that all students can be educated well in heterogeneous classes?

Part One describes the development of a vision and the alignment of stakeholders that a conversion effort requires. Chapter One argues for the need to create small autonomous schools and the role that conversion plays in this broader movement. Chapter Two presents an overview of the conversion process, outlining the leadership and technical tasks that it involves, and detailing planning, timing, and phasing of conversions. Chapter Three focuses on the district and its role in creating policy that supports the needs of small schools, such as new accountability systems that honor small school autonomy. It provides some examples of district change. Conversion involves the whole community, and Chapter Four presents an overview of stakeholder engagement and provides examples of how parents, students, and community organizations have led or been involved in conversion efforts.

Part Two shifts our focus from the broad picture of conversion to the small schools that are its objective. It discusses five main issues in founding and sustaining effective autonomous small schools. In Chapter Five we discuss how schools create their vision and identity, and how vision drives a school's design, instructional practice, and culture. Chapter Six discusses how teachers can be supported in developing pedagogical tools that work in small schools, and how helping teachers develop or enhance these competencies increases their support for the reform. Chapter Seven discusses implications for leadership in small schools, how to prepare new leaders, and how small school leadership differs from leadership in large comprehensive schools. Chapter Eight describes ways of designing a curriculum that prepares all students for postsecondary success, specifically looking at the challenges of electives and advanced placement courses. Multiple schools' sharing the same building creates its own challenges, which we discuss in Chapter Nine.

Part Three discusses the issues that arise in the transition from large schools to autonomous small schools. Chapter Ten presents our best thinking on rolling out or phasing in new schools; that is, the decision regarding how many schools to form, when to do so, and with what grade levels, among other key considerations. In Chapter Eleven we discuss how efforts have managed student assignment of new schools to balance issues of choice and equity. How teachers choose or are assigned to new schools is the topic of Chapter Twelve. We suggest a few core principles for thinking about the staffing process and for considering contractual issues. Finally, we return to the main vision and objectives of conversion work and share key considerations as you continue the work of creating your small autonomous schools in Chapter Thirteen. In our appendices we provide other resources to support the design and creation of autonomous small schools, including model guidelines for small schools and contact information for organizations and schools profiled in this book.

Acknowledgments

Various chapters in this book have benefited from criticism and commentary from friends and colleagues. We'd like to thank our colleagues at the Coalition of Essential Schools National Office—Abbey Kerins, Eva Frank, Jackie Gross, Jill Davidson, and Lewis Cohen for their close reading and expert advice, and Mara Benitez, Brett Bradshaw, Laura Flaxman, Carol Lind, and Shilpa Sood for their critical contributions and support. We are especially grateful to and would like to thank Charlotte Ciancio, who willingly volunteered her own time (and was not a captive audience in the same office) to read and offer feedback. We also thank Charlotte, as well as Marcy Raymond, Alison Byrd-English, and Paul Tytler for their incredible panel presentation at our session at the 2004 Coalition of Essential Schools Fall Forum. Thanks also to Edmund Gordon, a model educator who inspired Lisette, and to our editor, Christie Hakim, who guided us through this process.

In addition, we want to recognize all the school and community people who made time to share with us the reality of the work they were doing in schools and communities. We learned and benefited from each conversation. It's always a challenge to quote someone's words without the full context of a much longer conversation; we hope that we have captured the words of the people we've interviewed and the wisdom of their experience in a way that will resonate with them.

Our debt goes to Meg Anderson, Daniel Baron, Maureen Benson, Annmarie Boudreau, Sharon Brown, Dolores Caruso, John D'Anieri, Dan French, Gerry Garfin, Bill Gerstein, Holly Hanson, Bill Hart, Dina Heisler, Susan Hoeltzel, Megan Howey, Steve Jubb, Jamie Kane, Michelle Kennedy,

Michael Klonsky, Anna Le, Rick Lear, Jeff Liberty, Annie Lott, Ronny Mancuso, Chinyelu Martin, Brian McKibben, Venus Mesui, Gary Moed, Jack Mitchell, Larry Myatt, Eric Nadelstein, Laurie Olson, Jan Reeder, LaShawn Routé-Chatmon, John Sanchez, Holly Schoettlin, Kristen Scott-George, Steve Shapiro, Sue Showers, Max Silverman, Stephen Spring, Peter Steinberg, Daphannie Stephens, Steven Strull, Shael Suransky, Rosann Tung, John Welch, George Wood, George York, Jess Yurwitz, and Iris Zucker.

Our final thanks go to the thousands of students, parents, community members, and educators who work every day to make a difference in our schools.

The Coalition of Essential Schools

In 1984, Theodore R. Sizer and several colleagues published their findings from a five-year investigation of teaching, learning, and school design in *A Study of High Schools.* This seminal work found that despite variations in location and demographics, high schools in America were remarkably similar and simply inadequate. Wary of repeating the dismal historical record of major top-down reform initiatives, Sizer chose not to advocate reform based on a single vision or model for high schools. Instead, he identified a set of common principles, practices, and concepts for effective schools and teaching that each school community could implement according to its strengths and needs. A group of twelve schools in seven states agreed to redesign themselves on the basis of Sizer's ideas and to form the Coalition of Essential Schools. Since then, CES has grown into a network of hundreds of schools and more than twenty CES centers across the country. The network supports the continuous growth of large numbers of individual educators and the creation of schools that strive to fully enact CES principles—schools that emphasize equity, personalization, and intellectual vibrancy.

CES Schools

CES schools share a common set of beliefs about the purpose and practice of schooling, known as the CES Common Principles. Based on decades of research and practice, the principles call for all schools to offer

- Personalized instruction to address individual needs and interests
- Small schools and classrooms, where teachers and students know each other well and work in an atmosphere of trust and high expectations
- Multiple assessments based on performance of authentic tasks

- The achievement of equitable outcomes for students
- Democratic governance practices
- Close partnerships with the school's community

CES Centers

A CES center is an independent organization guided by the CES Common Principles, providing long-term professional development and technical assistance to schools. Centers work with schools to develop plans for change consistent with the principles. The exact requirements of membership vary from center to center and are responsive to the needs of local schools in their reform efforts.

CES National

CES National is the national voice of the Coalition. CES National supports the work done by CES teachers, schools, and centers by providing national networking opportunities; by promoting public engagement in issues of school reform; by conducting research; and by providing professional development. CES National seeks to ensure that successes in one region of the country are shared in other areas of the country. The CES national office is in Oakland, California. To learn more about the Coalition, please visit www.essentialschools.org.

The Authors

Jay Feldman is director of research at the Coalition of Essential Schools. He has conducted research in child development, whole school change, forms of democratic and equitable schooling, and alternative education. His interests include the educative functions of play and age-mixing, children's moral development, and understandings of race and diversity. He has a M.Ed. from the Harvard Graduate School of Education and a Ph.D. from Boston College in developmental psychology.

M. Lisette López is a senior program associate of the National Small Schools Project of the Coalition of Essential Schools. Prior to CES, Lisette led a range of action research, policy advocacy, and community-based education projects to help build the capacity of schools, youth programs, and community agencies to respond positively and equitably to diverse student populations and communities. She has an M.A. in education from U.C. Berkeley.

Katherine G. Simon earned her M.A. and Ph.D. in curriculum and teacher education from the Stanford University School of Education. Originally a high school English and drama teacher, she served as director of research and co-executive director of CES. Katherine is the author of *Moral Questions in the Classroom: How to Get Kids to Think Deeply About Real Life and Their School Work* (2001), which was named "outstanding book in curriculum for 2001-2002" by the American Education Research Association. She is also coauthor of *Questioning Practices: Inquiry into Student and Teacher Work* (2004). She currently leads workshops for school faculties on curriculum and instructional design and writes on parenting and school reform issues.

Part 1

Toward a Common Purpose

Chapter 1

Education for the Information Age

MOST OF US have had some experience—perhaps fleeting, and perhaps outside school—with the kind of learning that characterizes good schools: the hum of collaboration, of building, of creating; the sense of purpose; the excitement of new discovery. We cherish the sense of growth and development over time, not just one fascinating moment, and the warm human connections—people to ask for knowledge or for a hand, people with whom to laugh or commiserate. Such an environment makes participants willing to take risks, to stretch intellectually, because they share a collective commitment to support and honor such attempts, not only the outcomes. With such a sense of collective discovery and growth, it's not completely clear who are the learners and who are the teachers. In these experiences of learning, some of our deepest human needs—for meaning, connection, contribution, and growth—are met.

Such are the small schools we envision. We are confident they can exist, because such schools exist today. Our task is to convert all schools into this ideal. But we have a long way to go. Research on our current system of high schools paints a picture of failure:

- More than 90 percent of students from the top two income quartiles graduate from high school—compared to 65 percent of those from the bottom quartile (Mortenson, 2001).

- Only 28 percent of low-income students are enrolled in college preparatory curricula, compared to 49 percent of middle-income students and 65 percent of higher-income students (Gates Education Policy Paper, 2003).

- For every hundred students who begin the ninth grade, sixty-seven finish high school in four years; thirty-eight go to college, and only eighteen earn associate's degrees within three years or bachelor's degrees within six years (Mortenson, 2000).

- Only about 50 percent of African American and Latino ninth graders graduate from high school within four years, compared to 79 percent of Asian Americans and 72 percent of whites (Greene & Forster, 2003).

- U.S. workers with bachelor's degrees earn nearly a million dollars more over the course of a lifetime than those with only a high school diploma (U.S. Census Bureau, 2002).

A Vision of Education for the Twenty-First Century

So what do we need to do? What do successful high schools look like? In general, they have less than a hundred students at each grade level and less than four hundred overall. And smaller is better: the Coalition of Essential Schools believes in a ratio that allows each child to be known well; KnowledgeWorks argues for no more than seventy-five students in each grade, and for three hundred total students in a school. Successful schools are *autonomous*, that is, they control their own resources—budget, staffing, curriculum and assessment, governance and policies, and scheduling, consistent with state and district standards. Autonomy includes hiring and evaluation of teachers and staff consistent with labor contracts, and it also includes the freedom to set different school days and calendar years for both students and faculty in accordance with the school's own principles, as well as to create governance structures that give school staff increased decision-making powers over budget approval, principal selection and firing, and programs and policies. If a school shares a site with other programs, it does not have to seek permission of the site's cohabitants when it wants to change its programs—though it may have to negotiate site usage issues. (See Chapter Two for a description of specific autonomies.)

Nonetheless, successful schools differ greatly from one another. Their academic visions and missions are diverse. Some, like the Met School in Providence, Rhode Island, tailor their programs as closely as possible to the interests and passions of individual students, asking all students to spend extensive time in community internships, working as apprentices to a wide variety of professionals. Some, like the Boston Arts Academy in Massachusetts, organize coursework around a particular discipline or set of disciplines—in this case, the performance arts—and use these disciplines as a lens for academic learning. Some, like LaGuardia Middle College High in New York City, teach a traditional curriculum but provide such a high level of personalized attention that *every* student will be ready for college-level work by graduation.

This diversity of academic vision is rivaled by the diversity of physical settings. For the schools we need now, no single model defines what constitutes a viable physical plant. In some cases, where organizers have had the opportunity to design a facility with a particular educational philosophy in mind, schools look quite different from our standard image. The School of Environmental Studies (affectionately known as the "Zoo School") in suburban St. Paul, Minnesota, for example, looks more like the offices of a busy architectural firm. Each student's home base is an individual work station, and there are lots of comfortable niches of different sizes for collaboration. Other schools find their homes in converted storefronts, churches, grocery stores, and neighboring houses on a city street. Some tuck themselves into spare (or intentionally created) space in other civic buildings—the municipal art museum, city hall, the opera house, a recreation center in a large park . . .

Still other schools may look very much like what we currently think of as a high school, with wide, locker-lined halls leading to traditional-sized classrooms, a big lunch room, and a library. These schools result from a process called *conversion;* it's unsurprising that they still look like comprehensive high schools at first glance, because they're in a building that used to host one large high school that offered a wide variety of classes and electives. Now it hosts multiple new small autonomous schools with more specialized curricula, but the walls are the same as always. Schools that share a building may mingle with one another, but often they are *interconnected* instead, meaning they share a site but each has control over a contiguous space it can call its own. What makes them distinctive is that young people and adults know each other well. That's because the actual school population is small, and multiple independent schools share the same building. Their offerings are genuinely *new,* not a repackaged version of an existing program, not subsidiary to the larger school in any way, and not a model of the larger school's practices in a smaller format. They are qualitatively different organizations. At the Julia Richman Complex in New York City, for example, six schools, including a pre-K–8 special education school, a high school for new learners of English, and three other high schools, share space with a day-care center and a community medical center.

Despite their diversity of physical sites and curricular programs, the schools we need are small in size and share key convictions, goals, and methods. These are the essential elements common to all of the new schools:

- *Intellectual vibrancy:* A commitment to help all students tap into their love of learning and to prepare all students for postsecondary work. Theodore Sizer, founder of the Coalition of Essential Schools, writes, "The school should focus on helping young people learn to use their minds well." Our current system, with its college prep and regular tracks, assumes that not all students need the same level of intellectually challenging work or need to be ready for postsecondary education. In an Information Age economy, this is simply no longer viable. The new schools we envision will organize themselves to prepare all students to use their minds well and to attend college, if they so choose.

- *Personalization:* A commitment to nurture each student as an individual. In our current system, it is largely assumed that all students will be on the same page with all their peers every day, in every class. Everyone reads the same material; everyone does the same homework; everyone takes the same tests on the same day. This sameness does not match what we know about human cognition. The truth is that each of us learns differently. We each have our own set of passions, interests, and talents, and our own learning style. To nurture all students as individuals, no matter what their curricular focus, each new school will build in flexibility and responsiveness as part of the way it works. The structure allows staff to know students well. Students in all schools will be able to make choices about what they want to delve into in depth. Personalization enables schools to be responsive to a specific student's experiences and social and community context.

- *Equity:* A commitment to reverse embedded inequities. In our current system, poor students and students of color are far more likely to attend overcrowded schools with less skilled teachers and deteriorating facilities. Within any given school, they are more likely to be taught by the least skilled teachers in the most crowded classrooms (Center for the Future of Teaching and Learning, 2000). Our new schools, individually and collectively, will provide all students with the resources they need to receive an excellent education and will actively monitor student outcomes to ensure that all students are succeeding. Attending to personalization and intellectual vibrancy is pivotal to achieving equity.

Remaking an Icon

Most of us remember high school as a place of adolescent socialization, negotiating cliques and peer groups, waiting for the bell to ring so we could meet friends in the hallways. As the bricks and mortar of the large high school dominates the American landscape, the cultural image of the large comprehensive high school dominates America's collective identity. Either personally experienced or stamped on the collective consciousness through Hollywood's endless films, the image of a pack of young people moving, anonymous to teachers, from one class to another, sitting in rows of desks, listening to lectures, tracked according to perceived college aspirations (which generally means by socioeconomic and racial background) and struggling through adolescent challenges with their peers is something we all share.

The large comprehensive high school was conceived at the beginning of the twentieth century to fit an industrial society. These schools were originally expected to be a sorting mechanism for an economy that had a place for students who did not graduate. They were not intended to educate all students to the level of college readiness, and the system has always done a grave disservice to some children and communities. Comprehensive high schools have often unwittingly contributed to what Jonathon Kozol has called "savage inequalities" by tracking low-income students and children of color and being unresponsive to the needs and calls for accountability from their families and communities. Middle- and upper-class white students received an academically challenging college preparatory program, while predominantly lower-income students and students of color received business or vocational programs (from which a good number dropped out). These schools were founded on conceptions of teaching-as-information-delivery, conceptions that have been thoroughly debunked in the last generation of scholarship about human cognition.

The Bill & Melinda Gates Foundation, a driving force behind the creation of new small autonomous schools, offers five reasons why large comprehensive high schools fail to meet the needs of students:

- *Incoherence:* High schools offer a dizzying array of disconnected courses with little guidance.

- *Isolation:* Many teachers see more than 150 students daily. Both teachers and students have little adult contact.

- *Anonymity:* High schools have doubled in size in the last generation, resulting in overcrowding and reduced student and teacher interaction.

- *Low expectations:* Only one of the four to six tracks in most high schools prepares students for college.

- *Inertia:* High schools are slow to change due to large and isolated staffs, restrictive state and district policies and employment agreements, over-precise higher education entrance requirements, and an array of interest groups dictating much of school policy.

Students today must be prepared for a changing Information Age economy. According to Michelle Kennedy, a teacher who became teacher-leader of the Math, Science, and Technology Academy (MAST), a new autonomous school in the West Clermont Local School District in Cincinnati, Ohio:

> *People need to realize we're moving from the Industrial to the Information Era. Now people have to take the information that we have at our fingertips and evaluate and learn from it. It's a very different mindset. Few students can have a high-paying, successful job without going beyond a high school diploma, whether it is a skill, trade, two- or four-year degree, or beyond. And the hardest thing right now is to convince the community of that because our community's experience is "Well, all I have is a high school diploma and I have a decent paying job." But what was good enough for them is not going to be good enough for their children.*

Being prepared for the Information Age requires students to be analytical thinkers, effective communicators and problem solvers, and lifelong learners. Students should be prepared for being engaged members of an active democracy, which requires them to be knowledgeable, reflective, and able to embrace their civic responsibilities. They need an informed point of view, a meaningful knowledge of the world, a capacity to grapple with complex problems, and a willing ability to engage with people different from themselves.

The new expectation of high schools reflects a shift in the purpose of schooling and is in tension with the structures, cultures, and instructional strategies of today's schools. Compelled to consider options other than the status quo, many parents, teachers, superintendents, and business leaders have asked, What do our students need for the future to prepare them to have the opportunity to attend four-year colleges? What skills do they need to get an economically secure job or to become active citizens? What will enable disengaged youth to be leaders and revive their communities? Shared among the answers to these questions has been the conclusion that something dramatic must change in the whole system of providing education.

New York City has undertaken a large-scale questioning of the school system, concentrating first on district-wide reforms in the Bronx. According to Peter Steinberg, director of the Bronx New Century High Schools, "Everyone who has gone through this system (and most educational systems) believes that those systems don't effectively serve young people or their communities well." Steinberg observes, "One of the benefits for us working in the Bronx was that everyone believed that the educational system was not working." This community consensus led the district to make fundamental changes rather than just tinker around the edges.

Failing students or school districts are not the only concerns driving conversions. Bill Hart, principal of Leominster High School in Leominster, Massachusetts, echoes the idea that change is needed not only to serve students who currently drop out but to serve all students better. Few if any comprehensive high schools serve all their students well; fewer push even the highest-achieving students to really use their minds. Hart argues, "High schools traditionally have been very scholar-academic, and very teacher centered. I don't care how well your kids are doing, we are not preparing them for the world they need to be in if we aren't focusing—not only on how much information they can acquire and manipulate—but on how well they use their minds, focusing on critical thinking skills." When Hart speaks with parents of high-achieving students, he tells them, "Yes, your kid is doing well, but I'm in classrooms every single day and too often kids are passive recipients of information. Even though kids might be straight A students, if we haven't pushed them to use their minds in the most effective way, then we haven't given them the education they deserve. And you have a false comfort, thinking, because they are getting high grades, that they are getting the education they need and they deserve."

Many educators, parents, and others have concluded that today's large comprehensive high schools have unfixable flaws. While there have always been examples of small schools that served children well, the current form of secondary education has been remarkably stable and has lasted for over a century—in the face of repeated waves of reform. As Phillip Schlechty writes, "Public schools have no history of producing an entire population of academically well grounded citizens, despite the persistent myth of a golden age of education, [therefore] *if schools of America are to survive and thrive, American educators must be prepared to do things that have never been done, under conditions that have no precedents in our history*" (2001, p. 9, emphasis in original). This system must now give way to a new form of schooling.

Small Schools for a New Society

"Small schools can be the antidote to an educational system that has lost its soul as it has become more bureaucratic and impersonal. If teaching and learning above all are about the relationships constructed by teachers and learners—and I believe they are—then small schools hold out the promise of equality in education because they can promote the demanding but affirming personal relationships essential for high levels of student learning" (Nieto, 2000, p. 13).

The transformation of existing high schools into the small schools we need requires much more than changing school size. It requires a paradigm shift in the way that everyone—students, teachers, and a surprisingly wide range of community members—view what schools do, what they look like, what students need to know and experience as adolescents, how they really learn and how they should be taught. It requires giving up one vision and building another. The transformation of the physical large schools that stand behind the icon requires deep shifts in culturally embedded beliefs and in the actual institutionally embedded instruction, school design, and school culture.

Cotton (2001) notes five elements that are critical to the success of small schools:

- *Self-determination,* or the autonomy to make key decisions regarding space, time, budget, curriculum, instruction, and personnel

- *Identity,* which includes a clear mission and vision, thematic focus, and a focus on student achievement

- *Personalization,* or knowing students well, having heterogeneous classes in which each student's needs are met, and parent and community involvement and participation in the life of the school

- *Support for teaching,* including leadership and decision making, professional development, collaboration, and a large repertoire of instructional strategies

- *Functional accountability*—for students, using multiple forms of assessment, and for schools, providing two-way accountability with districts, school boards, and legislatures

Small autonomous schools can bring all five elements to bear, and they work. Indeed, research over the past fifteen years supports what educators have experienced: Students do better in autonomous small schools than in large comprehensive high schools. Small schools are safer, have greater teacher and parent satisfaction, higher achievement and graduation rates and lower dropout rates, higher student attendance, greater participation in extracurricular activities, reduced racial achievement gaps, and a deeper sense of student affiliation (Ancess, 2003; Ancess & Wichterle, 1999; Darling-Hammond, 1997; Darling-Hammond, Ancess, & Ort, 2002; Cotton, 1996, 2001; Wasley & Lear, 2001; Lee & Loeb, 2000; Wasley et al., 2000; Howley, Strange, & Bickel, 2000; Raywid, 1996, 1999; Cushman, 1999; Klonsky & Klonsky, 1999; Lashway, 1998–1999; Fine, 1998; Gladden, 1998; Lee, Smith, & Croninger, 1995; Bryk & Thum, 1989; Center for Collaborative Education, 2004).

Small autonomous schools have also been found to be more effective than *small learning communities,* that is, individualized units that allow teachers and students to spend some time together within a larger high school, but without the autonomy of independent school status (U.S. Department of Education, 2001; Cotton, 2001; Gregory, 2001). Although small learning communities have been found to be effective to the extent that they have the conditions that are critical to small autonomous school success, as Gregory notes, it is common for small learning communities to revert to big-school strategies and lose much of the autonomy that makes them successful.

Creating Small Schools from Large Buildings

The infrastructure of secondary education in this country overwhelmingly consists of large school buildings. To take advantage of these facilities and spare the expense of building new ones, schools and districts are electing in ever-increasing numbers to undergo conversion of their large comprehensive high school buildings into several smaller autonomous schools—rather than start new schools from scratch. Even small-school proponents who believe that start-up schools face fewer obstacles than conversions acknowledge that the transformation of existing schools is essential if we are going to create enough small schools to serve all students. There is a broad sense that conversion, though difficult, is necessary. In the words of Larry Myatt, co-founder of Fenway High School in Boston and current provider of professional development to school leaders in the Boston Public School District Office of High School Renewal, "It's got to get done, there's no question about it. The prevalent reality around the nation is these are the schools that we have and we've got to start doing this [conversion] work."

At some schools, the first steps in the conversion journey have been championed by groups of parents who were fed up with the persistent failure of their local school system. In other areas, the process started with thoughtful educators concerned that only a small group of their students were learning to use their minds to their fullest potential. Some districts have initiated major strategic overhauls because of unacceptable racial achievement gaps. Elsewhere, principals have realized that they were losing students to charter or private schools as choice policies increased the number of alternatives available to students. In New York City, for example, community engagement paved the way for the planned creation of two hundred small schools.

Further, forming multiple small schools in a district is changing the structure of education from a comprehensive high school to a comprehensive system of small schools, which increases options for children. These schools all have the goal of preparing children for postsecondary education, but the specifics need to be determined within each district and school. For example, the Gates Foundation's Web site describes the objective for children and families to have choices from a "diverse portfolio of schools, each with different emphases, teaching approaches, and philosophies, all of which would prepare every student for college."

Few research studies have examined the experiences of students in converted high schools. A report on schools in their first year of conversion (American Institutes for Research & SRI International, 2004) found that students in converted schools appear to be doing well, but the schools face many complex and challenging problems before institutionalizing and sustaining success. This study reports that students in converted schools are known and cared about to a greater degree than in larger comprehensive schools and that parent-school communication is greater and more effective. Reports on student achievement were mixed: some students felt more academically challenged while others found schoolwork easier. Clearly, this is a work in progress as the evaluation examines schools in their first year of conversion. Still, the results are promising.

Guiding Principles of Conversion

In Oakland, San Diego, Sacramento, and San Mateo, California, in Boston and Worcester, Massachusetts, in Portland, Oregon, in Seattle and SeaTac, Washington, in St. Paul, Minnesota, in Chicago, Illinois, in East Cleveland and Cincinnati, Ohio, in Denver and Adams County, Colorado, and in many more districts coast to coast, schools are at some stage of converting from large to small. Schools are grappling with issues from whether they should transform a large school into small schools to crafting a design for each school, staging the opening of each school, and having each school fully emerge into its own. This book itself is a snapshot, written while work is still very much in process. It is an up-to-the-minute account of what we see as the most promising practices for school conversion.

We discuss common and vexing challenges that arise in school conversion and redesign efforts, detail stories from the field, and discuss the opportunities for gain and loss that the conversion process provides, while identifying some pitfalls often encountered along the way. We draw lessons from the literature of effective school design, school reform, and organizational development. We've interviewed more than seventy district personnel, technical assistance intermediaries, professional development coaches, principals, teacher-leaders, and community partners about their strategies for conversion, the challenges they have faced, and the central lessons they have learned. We have attempted to capture the best thinking on their experiences in their journey from large school to small.

We have heard a common thread in our conversations with school and community members across the country: *High schools must educate every student to the level of college readiness, for productive work in an information society and for active citizenship in a diverse society.* As we noted at the beginning of the chapter, society has fewer and fewer openings for people who emerge from school without that sort of education, and we are obligated to provide all students with the ability to support themselves and contribute to society. High schools need to educate all students to the same high level, and conversion efforts must develop a common understanding of why all students need to do well, what students need to be able to do, and how this change in thinking represents a paradigm shift for high school structure, culture, and instruction.

This overarching goal and the new call it places on high schools—to expect and educate all students to reach high outcomes—reflects a historical shift in the purpose of the institution of high school. It has two core implications for conversion.

Implication #1: Conversion is about radical transformation. A historical shift in the purpose of the institution of high school necessitates a parallel historical shift in the design of high schools and districts. Reforms that tweak, compromise, try to build on, and do not fundamentally remake dominant school culture, structure, instructional practice, and district relationships will fall short of meeting the needs we have of our high schools.

Implication #2: The biggest challenges are human, not technical. Any group of people will be somewhat resistant to or fearful of dramatic change. As the radical transformation of high schools involves change central to their social experience, core profession, and workplace, even more reluctance or resistance is natural. Though the technical tasks involved in converting a large school to several small ones are considerable, the human dimensions to this process loom even larger. Leading conversion requires an understanding of the connections and the differences between human and technical stages, tasks, and challenges—and how that human aspect is embedded in technical decisions.

Chapter 2
Leading the Process

WHEN CHARLOTTE CIANCIO became superintendent of the Mapleton Public Schools in Adams County, Colorado, almost half of its eighth grade graduating class was choosing to go to other districts for high school. (Colorado is an open enrollment state, so students can go anywhere they please if they provide their own transportation.) Students at Skyview High School, which has a population of more than twelve hundred students, 49 percent of whom are white, 45 percent Hispanic, and 23 percent eligible for free or reduced-price lunch, were faring poorly on the high-stakes state-mandated test. (Note: All demographic data in this book are from www.nces.ed.gov and represent the 2002–2003 school year.) Ciancio understood that the district needed to change, so one of her first activities was to involve the community in developing a strategic plan. They created a district vision statement that guaranteed that Mapleton's students would achieve their dreams, with the commitment that the district would provide students with an "enticing menu of learning opportunities."

The community engaged in data-based analysis to determine strengths and challenges in realizing this vision. According to Ciancio, "We analyzed the gap from where we are today to where we want to be. And there is quite a gap in Mapleton. We figured that to close that gap we were going to have to take some pretty dramatic and drastic measures. The good news for us is that as a whole community we want more than we were giving ourselves, more than we were giving our children. Nobody's satisfied with the results. I don't think anybody could stand and say what we're doing is good enough." Mapleton created a strategic plan that would enable them to enact their vision of education. The plan was to expand choice in the district by reinventing their one large comprehensive high school as six small autonomous schools, with a wide array of approaches to help students meet their potential.

• • •

As we noted in the Preface, many of the educators we interviewed asked us to emphasize that conversion is hard work. It usually involves making drastic changes to a moving target: developing new teaching techniques, implementing innovative school designs, retooling relationships, and refashioning school culture, all while continuing to work in the same facility with the same colleagues and meeting the needs of current students.

While educators emphasize the challenges of their work, they also ask us to convey their passion for the task. They are dedicated to giving students something better, to ensuring that students have what they need to succeed. This chapter outlines what we have learned about the timing and technical tasks of different phases of conversion work, and about the benefits of beginning as Charlotte Ciancio did by collaboratively developing a clear vision and a sound strategic plan.

Conversion Phases

> This reform redefines people's roles and responsibilities and you can't do that in a fast way, you have to grow that organically. If you try and force structural change it generates lots and lots of resistance, which diverts you from what the structural change is meant to do.
>
> —SHAEL SURANSKY,
> director of Bronx International High School in New York City

> There are certain conversations that have to happen. They're either going to be easy or hard but they come along in the process.
>
> —SHARON BROWN,
> external coach of Shaw High School in East Cleveland, Ohio

These words echo what we have heard in many conversations and observed among those involved in conversion efforts. As Richard Elmore writes, "The term 'control' applied to school improvement is a dubious concept" (2000,

p. 14). "The knowledge required for improvement must inevitably reside in the people who deliver instruction not in the people who manage them," he adds, so those leading change initiatives cannot control improvement or force changes as much as guide and provide direction.

Building on this notion, a key lesson that we learned is that the process of transformation appears to have key phases that leaders can anticipate and will need to guide and ultimately structure into their plans. Certain conversations, tasks, and steps turn out to be central and unavoidable. When done superficially or not done early enough, they can become obstacles or drags to the transformation process. Clearly, in so complex an undertaking, the phasing of individual initiatives will vary according to the needs and resources of the local context, but a broad overview helps to frame the flow of the work in three phases:

1. *Vision, Explore, and Engage:* The effort begins with the creation of a broad-based vision, a strategic plan, and a structure for the work among multiple stakeholders.

2. *Design:* The design process requires the creation and support of design teams, along with the development of capacity for creating the small schools, making the transition, and supporting the new schools from the district level.

3. *Implementation:* Once new autonomous schools open, schools and districts must continue to build capacity to support them. School and community members deal with the effects of the change, such as creating new relationships among adults and between adults and students, as they create and implement new systems and structures.

Vision, Explore, and Engage

Mapleton—the district featured in the story that opens this chapter—is an example of a clear, thoughtful beginning to conversion. Faced with the need to transform her district, Ciancio coordinated what appear to be key elements of the process: naming the problems in the current situation, building an understanding of how best to educate children, conveying that knowledge, and creating the will to do something about it. A necessary and ideally early step in conversion is acknowledgment and naming of the problem—we are not adequately educating our children. Stakeholders—parents, students, teachers, community members, and others—realize that too many students are dropping out of high school or too few are being intellectually challenged. All begin to recognize that there probably is a better way to reach all students and teach them well. The exploration, then, is focused on the best mechanism to address the defined problem. Conversion is one option for this mechanism.

During this time, stakeholders can share their beliefs and aspirations, listen to different perspectives and points of view, and weigh choices and trade-offs. The discussion is about getting the schools that you need and serving students well. It is about creating that shared understanding of the problem. Although schools may have a vision to change in a specific way, we recommend that stakeholder engagement be an open-ended process that allows for the possibility of different outcomes. Engagement is not simply about accepting or fighting the idea of converting the larger high school to small autonomous schools. If the discussions are already about preset options, then stakeholders will recognize that they have been left out of the process. School communities decide to create small autonomous schools because they feel they are the best vehicle to meet the needs of their students and create equitable and excellent schools. It is important for stakeholders to agree and understand that there needs to and will be a fundamental shift in the way that we educate children; this is not reform on the margins. We discuss the role of stakeholders in more depth in Chapter Four.

As we know from trying to create and sustain much simpler changes in school life, schools, like all institutions, are resistant to change. Because the movement to small autonomous schools is a reinvention, creating and holding a vision for the change is a vital part of the process; it is particularly important in the first stage, which some educators have referred to as the "why convert" stage. A shared vision is based on shared images of the future you wish to create. In the face of stress, the shared vision provides a rudder to keep the change process on course. "Troubles and stresses and petty conflicts can appear more trivial in light of a compelling shared vision. Without a pull toward some goal which people truly want to achieve, the forces in support of the status quo can be overwhelming" (Senge, 1990, p. 209).

Creating a vision and mission lays a foundation for the later work that needs to be done. This minimizes the need to revisit the issue of "Why?" later, thus minimizing the time such questioning will take. It also provides focus and leverage—when, as often happens, one group's commitment begins to weaken, others know why it is important to step in. It is an opportunity to self-reflect and deepen knowledge about the strengths and challenges of the school. This develops the participants' collective ability to self-analyze and plan strategically, an important skill that drives and sustains change work. In addition, the shared vision and mission help everyone manage the day-to-day complexities of change.

The research indicates that most conversion efforts find themselves facing strong pressure to be driven by day-to-day decisions in the face of insufficient time and resources and constant complexity and crises. When a group of people are attuned to their collective vision, they are more likely to stay connected to the students' needs and their long-range conversion goals. They are less likely to be derailed by the day-to-day challenges conversion presents along the way. To be successful in radically transforming a school, a wide range of people need to muster a deep commitment to and ownership for the change. Vision gives those involved a sense of purpose, identifies compelling reasons, defines understandable goals for each action. When the vision is clear about the *why* of conversion and the need for a small school, the tasks of conversion and school design are made easier.

Researchers who have studied change in schools, such as Fullan (2001) and Evans (1996), and in a range of organizations, including Kotter (1996) and Senge (1990; Senge, Cambron-McCabe, Lucas, Smith, & Dutton, 2000), believe that leadership is also fundamental to keeping change efforts and organizations on track. Effective leadership both resembles and supports a clear shared vision; it works to prevent the pressure and complexity of day-to-day decisions from derailing the conversion. Leadership, as distinct from management, focuses on guiding change. Leaders avoid becoming so mired in managing the change that the ultimate vision and goals of conversion are lost. In the Mapleton School District, Charlotte Ciancio heads a leadership team that meets regularly to deal with the many details of the task within the context of their whole vision. Their focus is guided by a strategic plan that was developed with the community. The goal the district defined—increasing choices for students—is a rudder guiding their decisions as they encounter roadblocks and work to create small autonomous schools of different sizes and visions that provide engaging but distinct learning environments for students.

Exploration Stage Activities

During the exploration stage, most conversion efforts benefit by the creation of a leadership team that includes people from all stakeholder groups (district staff, school staff, parents and community members, and students) to oversee the process. The leadership team's first task is information gathering. Members investigate their own school setup and results (through an analysis of school-based data and creation of a school portfolio), research the literature on small schools, and visit other small schools to see what they look like, how they function, what and how they choose to teach, and so on. These visits often prove to be what brings the whole process to life; nothing brings home the worth of the effort like a chance to see success in action.

Once the team develops a general idea of the process, it should engage the broader community through such measures as public forums, student- and parent-facilitated meetings, presentations to the school board, and partnerships with non-school agencies. (It is often useful to hire a public relations firm to provide expertise to the district in communicating with stakeholder groups.)

The next step is to create a Memorandum of Understanding (MOU) among key constituents to detail the factors that guide the school and district to a vision that supports effective small schools. MOUs typically include provisions that cover the following issues:

- School culture

  Personalization for students

  Collaboration among teachers

  High expectations for everyone

  Authentic student, parent, community engagement

  Respect and responsibility

  Distributed leadership

- Instruction and curriculum

  Performance-based assessment

  Personalized learning

- School design

- Size

- Autonomies

- District responsibilities

  A clearly defined system of central office support of small school design and implementation

Once the MOU is established, the team's next tasks are to create an internal and external communications plan and a strategic planning document. It should then engage staff in professional development to build capacity for the instructional strategies appropriate to small schools and create a plan for supporting leaders of small schools.

Throughout the process, the team should brainstorm the particular challenges that its site will face (such as district policy and difficulty of acquiring autonomy in specific areas) and create teams or committees to explore these challenges. It should partner with community organizations wherever feasible to enlist the broadest possible support for the conversion.

As an example, here is one way to structure the exploration process. The KnowledgeWorks Foundation, which provides both financial support and technical assistance to Ohio high schools interested in creating new small autonomous schools, uses a support process that contains many of these exploration activities. In the exploration stage, KnowledgeWorks schools:

1. Conduct a directed self-analysis of data.

2. Create a strategic plan, which includes creating and presenting a school portfolio, including plans to convert to autonomous small schools.

3. Engage with the community, discussing the role and function of high schools.

Schools create a school-based portfolio that examines the effectiveness of the school in meeting student, parent, and teacher needs. It turns out that using data to understand the school and students is an important step toward creating, believing in, and holding to a vision of reform. As schools create their portfolios in seven areas—student achievement, leadership, quality planning, professional development, information and analysis, continuous improvement and evaluation, and partnership and community engagement—they also create a strategic plan that addresses the gaps between where they are and where they would like to be.

In addition, KnowledgeWorks requires that each school partner with what they call a "Center of Strength": a community organization that receives funding and engages the community in multiple forums—at least twenty during the year—about high school education. The Center also becomes a key player in designing and supporting the creation of the small schools, if the decision is to move in that direction. This community engagement is parallel to and influences the school's portfolio and analysis. (See Exhibit 2.1 for a description of the basic principles implemented by the KnowledgeWorks Foundation.)

Planning Strategically

As stakeholders come together around a vision of education in which conversion has a central role, developing a plan that takes into account the considerable technical, leadership, and management tasks to make it a reality is an important next step. Large-scale change efforts that have been successful, and the conversion efforts that have the most promising practices, are aided by a strategic planning process. Strategic planning is important; as the saying goes, "Prior planning promotes proper performance." A strategic plan clearly defines the purpose of the change process and establishes realistic goals and objectives consistent with that change mission. It defines a clear time frame for change that is within the organization's capacity to implement.

EXHIBIT 2.1

Knowledgeworks' Fifteen Nonnegotiable Elements for Small School Design

1. Autonomous governance, budgets, structures, and staffing; flexible use of resources

2. Distributed leadership

3. Open access and choice for students

4. Identification of and release time for principal in first year of implementation

5. Professional development that clearly links changes in teaching practice to improved student achievement

6. A clearly defined system of central office support of small school design and implementation

7. A curriculum clearly aligned with state standards and focused on helping students use their minds well

8. Nontraditional scheduling that promotes deep student learning and meaningful relationships with teachers

9. Clearly demonstrated use of technology and advanced communications resources

10. Clearly stated benchmarks for improved student achievement

11. Performance assessment for students

12. Authentic community engagement (as defined by substantive community conversations that engage a broad array of stakeholders) that connects with and influences official decisions

13. Clear community involvement in the daily life of the school

14. Individual teacher advisers for each student

15. Target maximum population of four hundred students

Of course, no plan is ever perfect. Educators can only do their best at strategic thinking and implementation, continually learning from prior efforts, making adjustments to enhance the effectiveness of their work along the way. Initiatives that proceeded relatively well planned backwards from their vision, using concrete data and information they had gathered about their own context. They integrated this information with research and knowledge about effective school design and the lessons of school and organizational change. Investing the time to develop a strategic plan appears to have enabled what is an intense organizational change endeavor to achieve and sustain a vision and avoid having the press of work—their own desires for quickly remedying inequities—override capacity and obstruct the effort.

Strategic planning divides readily into two steps: Where are you now? and Where are you going? These steps help keep conversions on track by helping participants keep the big picture and vision in mind, even as they delve into extremely complex and challenging tasks.

1. *Where are you now?* Assess your school context in relevant areas.

Knowing from where and with what you are starting is a critical step. We have seen initiatives whose forward movement has been significantly hampered because the group failed to conduct an assessment of key aspects of current practice or attitudes. Insufficient assessments or understanding at the outset can lead to delays to the conversion later on. For example, one effort was almost blocked by community members because reform leaders underestimated the community's emotional attachment to the existing school even though it was one of the lowest performing in the state. Reform leaders had not taken the time to involve the community in discussions about educational vision and change. In another instance, a plan was based on the incorrect assumption that teachers supported the change. By not taking into account teachers' actual strengths, skill levels, and attitudes about the change, the plan led to delays as the team backtracked to build consensus and capacity among teachers.

A group might start by describing key aspects of current school structure, culture, relationships, practices, or attitudes that will need to change or be expanded on for conversion work. Resources for assessing relevant areas of school practice and stakeholder attitudes include Victoria Bernhardt's School Portfolio (1994), in which schools continually assess their practice in seven areas. In addition to thinking about the school, it is also necessary to assess current district policies, contracts, and regulations.

2. *Where are you going?* Envision short- and long-term goals.

The complexity of the conversion process makes it hard to be clear about the short- and long-term goals of conversion at the outset. Yet our informants tell us that defining specific objectives is crucial for future success—even though these goals evolve during the process. Goals-based planning starts with focus on the organization's mission and vision. Goals are defined in terms of the overall accomplishments the organization should achieve.

Here are some of the key questions to guide goal development:

What vision of small autonomous schools and conversion will best meet the needs of students in your community?

What specific instructional strategies will achieve the mission for your community of students?

What will the teaching look like in the schools that develop from your conversion? (See Chapter Five.)

How can teachers be supported in developing the pedagogical tools that work best in small schools? (See Chapter Six.)

How will working and learning in those schools feel?

What strategies will you use for creating effective youth and adult relationships, school culture, and community ties that support and enable success with your students?

What leadership structures will best support your teachers' instructional practice? (See Chapter Seven.)

What relationship with the district, changes in district policies, and autonomies are needed to allow the schools envisioned to do their work? (See Chapter Three.)

How can you design a curriculum that prepares all students for post-secondary success? (See Chapter Eight.)

Some efforts have successfully begun by envisioning what their ideal graduate would look like. This allows for an easy transition into thinking about how instruction would look different, and then into thinking about how instruction drives structural issues.

A number of conversion initiatives have lacked clarity about key components of their process; confusion about the range of autonomies that would be necessary to implement effective teaching strategies or a curricular vision, for example, was common. To avoid confusion or the possibility of drifting from the original mission of a conversion, it appears to be important that initiatives develop a clear and widely shared understanding of how students in the new small autonomous schools will be served well, and what policies and practices will be necessary to support student achievement.

Surfacing Underlying Beliefs

Much of what we have discussed involves stakeholders' communicating with one another about their beliefs. As noted by Sarason (1991) with regard to other reform efforts, effective school reform requires fundamental shifts in the way people think and interact, and it requires people to recognize unseen values and attitudes about power, privilege, and knowledge that keep existing structures, regulations, and authority relationships in place. According to Larry Myatt (who is currently a headmaster on assignment for the Office of High School Renewal in Boston), conversion involves such an unearthing and change in beliefs, attitudes, and practices, not just a process of creating them such as in new small schools. As Myatt has found, "Conversion high school work and small high school work are really different. . . . Conversion work is basically deconstruction—if you're really lucky and really successful you'll begin to deconstruct the old set of realities, all the paradigms. . . . That's much of the work, the deconstruction work."

It is necessary to make individual beliefs, visions, and assumptions explicit before shared ones can guide conversion work. This often involves surfacing beliefs that are unconsciously held or difficult to discuss. Members of the school community need to share personal visions, beliefs, and experiences about what constitutes a good school or whether all students have the ability to be prepared for college. These ideas are based on a wider and often more deeply held set of assumptions, values, and experiences. A shared vision is then based on shared values and images of the future for youth you wish to create.

Our research indicates that all conversion efforts have had to grapple on some level with individual beliefs or assumptions before reaching a consensus on these points:

- All students—regardless of their initial skill and motivation level or background—are capable of being prepared to enroll and succeed in college.

- Students at different levels can be taught successfully in the same classroom—for example, differentiated instruction in a classroom can really replace Honors and Advanced Placement (AP) courses and serve the needs of below-skill-level students without endangering those who would have been assigned to the advanced classes.

- Teaching conditions will improve—for example, schedule changes and collaboration actually increase and do not decrease the proportion of constructive work in the school day and the sense of autonomy a teacher feels.

Stakeholders can have some commonsense reasons to be dubious and question the premises and goals of conversion. For example, teachers and students may lack knowledge of what is involved in the change to small schools. This lack of knowledge can generate fear and strengthen loyalty to what exists. Fears may relate to concern about, for example, a teacher's capacity to work well with new instructional methods, in a new work environment, or with new systems of being evaluated. Members of the school community may also have concrete reasons to be committed to the school structure as it exists. Teachers and students may be loyal to instructional methods that have been successful for them, such as AP classes, even if they were not effective for all students. Other school members may not believe the type of change conceived of is really possible. One way that various points of resistance to change can be shifted is by educating stakeholders about small schools and their advantages, communicating with them about the conversion process and its consequences, or by visiting schools that work. Simultaneously building their capacity in the actual skills required for small autonomous schools has proven crucial (see Chapter Six on professional development for instruction).

Design

The implementation of the reform has a goal—the creation of multiple autonomous small schools. Ideally this goal comes clearly into focus for a number of constituents in the change process during the exploration period. In some instances, as when the KnowledgeWorks Foundation provides both funding and technical support to conversion efforts, many aspects of what the new autonomous small schools will look like are written explicitly into the grant and provided to the schools and districts as nonnegotiables (as shown in Exhibit 2.1). KnowledgeWorks believes that community agreement on these points is vital to a successful effort. In other instances, as in Indianapolis, Indiana, what the new schools and the district will look like is based upon a co-construction process that involves a partnership and agreement with multiple stakeholders, rather than having pieces seem to be imposed from the outside. For example, the Indianapolis team's list of necessary school attributes included personalization, common focus (adopting a consistent evidence-based instructional approach based on shared beliefs about teaching and learning), scheduled time for teachers to collaborate, and parent and community engagement. Necessary district attributes included decentralizing resources to allow flexibility and decision making as close to the small school and students as possible, removing obstacles to decision making, and providing adequate time and resources for personalized scheduling, professional development, and collaboration.

Agreeing on a vision gives all the key constituent groups a framework for moving forward with the conversion process. In this phase, conversion efforts need to plan the design, transition, and initial opening of autonomous small schools. The experience of the educators we surveyed indicates that it is also important to begin planning at the district level to support the new kind of schools.

The intensity and comprehensiveness of the design phase has a huge impact on the success of the implementation phase. Creating new small autonomous schools from a large school involves a variety of technical tasks. Some of these tasks are continuous—it is important that their planning is begun early in the process and their implementation does not end with the creation of autonomous schools. Continuous tasks focus on building the capacity of the individual, school, and district. For example, small school directors require a different skill set from that of traditional large school principals, needing a very generalized skill set but also a deep understanding of instructional practices that support, for example, the heterogeneous classrooms and inclusion practices that small schools use so effectively. Districts can begin to develop a new group of leaders from the beginning of their commitment to small schools.

Other tasks are discrete—they are specific to conversion and once implemented, do not occur again, although they are quite complex as well. For example, creating a roll-out plan for the new schools—the timing, the location, the size, the way each will open initially—is a complex task, but once all Grade 9–12 schools are formed, roll-out is complete. Table 2.1 summarizes

TABLE 2.1

Conversion Phases

Stage	Key Objectives	Conversion Leadership Team	Small School Design Team	Small School Staff
Vision, Explore, and Engage	Assess current situation Name the problem Develop shared understanding of the problem Develop shared vision for the strategy to address the problem Develop strategic plan	Include all stakeholder groups Data analysis Portfolio Visit small schools Internal/external communications plan (e.g. community forums) Organize staff professional development Create district policy teams Develop leadership Finalize MOU that captures shared vision Prepare communication plan		

Stage	Key Objectives	Conversion Leadership Team	Small School Design Team	Small School Staff
Design (Small Schools Creation and Selection)	Generate and select the designs	Support design teams Finalize proposal or design development, evaluation, and decision process	Include all stakeholder groups Create small school vision Develop community partnerships Create proposal	
Design (Small Schools Transition)	Develop initial plan for rolling out selected designs Finalize details of roll-out plan and comprehensive system of autonomous small schools	Phase out large school control of new autonomous schools Transition large school leaders Support small school staff Phase in roll-out decisions		Design schedule, pedagogical practices, curricular identity Hire staff Develop communication and recruiting plan Develop strategic plan
Design (District Transformation)	Create district policies that support small schools (for example, autonomies, accountability)	Organize staff professional development Work with district policy teams Develop small school leadership Develop student and teacher assignment policies Negotiate contractual issues		Select leadership Design governance Conduct continued professional development
Implementation	Open small autonomous schools Implement new district policies			Finalize Building Council Finalize decision-making process and structure Operate continuous improvement plan

the tasks we have identified from our research. If you set up a similar table for your own district, you can extend it to include the roles of district staff, parents, students, and community groups as well. In the following chapters, we discuss these tasks, describing the main issues related to each of them and how different efforts have addressed them.

For a more detailed list of the tasks and decisions involved, sorted out by which ones require effort throughout the conversion process and which can be done once and allowed to stand, see Appendix E. Feel free to photocopy it as a ready reference for the conversion team.

We see three phases within the design phase:

- *Small schools creation and selection:* Creating and supporting teams that design specific schools

- *Small schools transition and initiation:* Creating the processes, policies, and documents needed by each school

- *District transformation:* Creating district policies that support small schools

Small Schools Creation and Selection

Goals of this phase often include creating the best designs to serve as foundations for creating effective schools, engaging and building ownership among multiple stakeholders, and constructing a manageable process for supporting this work. Most conversion efforts use some type of design team to manage the process, assembling a group of people from a wide range of constituencies to be responsible for creating the mission, vision, structure, and focus of each new small and autonomous school. Here are six key questions to keep in mind when thinking about creating and supporting design teams:

- How will each design team be created?
- Who should be on the design teams?
- What guides the design process?
- How many design teams should there be?
- How will the design teams be supported?
- How are proposals evaluated, and by whom?

How are design teams created? Design teams have been formed by many approaches, such as by a Request for Proposals (RFP) process, through assignment, or an open-space technology approach. Most efforts use RFPs or a similar formal process in which any group of teachers can join together and design a new school. In multi–high school districts, an RFP can even let teachers from different schools form a design team together.

Here is one process that proved effective: In a two-hour after-school meeting that included school staff, parents, community people, district office, middle school teachers, and students, a school used an open-space technology process to help clarify what was possible and desirable. Anyone attending the meeting could propose an idea and then see if people wanted to join them. Seventeen themes were proposed and twelve proposals were laid out. This school had designed a "think sheet"—a grid with the requirements for each school. The design conversations were focused on some of those requirements. Groups presented their initial ideas and posted them in a gallery walk, where each group could observe other groups' work and provide feedback. Then everyone was randomly regrouped and each of the new small groups had to pick the four ideas that they thought would be best for the students in that school and that community. At the end of the session, some consensus began to emerge about what ideas would satisfy the requirements identified as essential to meet the needs of their students.

Who should be on a design team? We believe that design teams should have representatives from multiple constituencies—school staff, district staff, parents, community members, and students. Involving all members of the school community holds the potential for building support for the new schools, creating schools that meet everyone's needs, and developing mutually beneficial partnerships. However, many schools feel that not every teacher has to be on a design team, nor is every teacher willing to be on one. If not every teacher is on a design team, the conversion effort will need a process for bringing the rest of the teachers on board, getting them to commit to the work that has occurred, and eventually to develop a sense of ownership.

What guides the design process? Districts and schools have defined certain criteria for design teams to meet, and this is effective in that it frames what components teams think about in the design process. We believe that small school formation is greatly enhanced by examining any of a number of well-constructed models or sets of principles to guide and assess effective small schools. Among these are the Common Principles of the Coalition of Essential Schools, which were developed twenty years ago and are a foundation for many effective high schools, and the seven attributes of high-achieving schools identified through an intensive research review by the Bill & Melinda Gates Foundation, which guides their considerable grant-making for small schools. Building on the work of National Association of Secondary School Principals in collaboration with the Educational Alliance at Brown University (which resulted in *Breaking Ranks* and *Breaking Ranks II*), the School Redesign Network (SRN) at Stanford University, developed with the leadership of Linda Darling-Hammond, has identified ten features of effective small schools. See Appendix D for the lists of principles and attributes mentioned in this paragraph.

When KnowledgeWorks takes part in a small school development effort, it requires that the design teams create five specific products. Creating these products serves to guide the teams into designing effective schools.

1. *Instructional Identity:* The team needs to develop an organizing framework for how their school will teach students and improve the learning process. They can explore frameworks such as multiple intelligences or learning exhibitions. The resulting school need not teach entirely within this framework, but its people do need to develop expertise in the organizing principle they choose.

2. *Communications and Marketing Plan:* Each proposed school must have a name, a tag line, and an internal and external communications strategic plan, including how its sponsors will publicize the school's identity so students and parents can make meaningful choices. Preparing this plan also helps a school determine and articulate its identity.

3. *Instructional Program:* The team needs a plan for how to facilitate student development with personalization and academic rigor. Each small school addresses an essential question: How are we going to encourage the development of each child from ninth grade to twelfth grade using our instructional identity as an organizing framework? Schools do this through critically examining their graduation requirements, their use of time, the progress that each child will have to demonstrate, and the strategy for personalizing instructional practice. (Typical question: "Here's how this child is doing today—so how do I change what I do to help make tomorrow's performance better?")

4. *Small School Strategic Plan:* Few of today's large schools can say they prepare all students for postsecondary education, which is a stated goal of the new small schools. The team needs to specify how they will close the gaps within the new schools over the next two years.

5. *Literacy Plan:* Related to the strategic plan, the team needs a description of how the school will support students' literacy development, particularly those students who need extra support.

How many design teams should there be? Should there be more design teams than the number of schools expected to be created? The goal is to create the best schools possible and provide appropriate support for the design teams involved. If the numbers are the same, then it is in everyone's best interest that all the teams succeed, and they all need support throughout the process. If there are more teams than planned schools, then some will be winners and others losers. Some teams will not make the cut, but the best designs and strongest teams will be selected, increasing the chance that the best schools will emerge. This places pressures on teams to develop strong proposals and create a buzz about their ideas. In other efforts, design teams working on similar visions were asked if they wanted to combine. Some districts used straw polls of teachers and students to help teams refine their vision to better meet their school community's needs.

Conversion efforts often decide on the number of schools they wish to create before design teams are formed. This has the benefit of making the process simpler, but may limit potential options and configurations of schools.

How are design teams supported? Design teams have three specific support needs. First, they need support in understanding effective design to shape school vision, instructional practice, school design, and leadership structure to plan the most effective and equitable school for local needs and context. Often the criteria included in the RFP or similar document provide the basic requirements and standards that they need to address to begin to create effective designs. Second, design teams need time and resources to meet and plan and involve multiple stakeholders in the process. Team members need to be able to collaborate, acquire information, and deepen their relationships with one another. Some efforts have been able to support design team leaders with full or partial time released from other responsibilities, while others have provided release time or collaborative time during the day. Third, design teams need support in developing their capacity to work effectively in small schools, such as a deeper understanding of how to use the small school autonomies.

Support requires careful thought to avoid the appearance of inequity. It's unfortunately easy to get things wrong. In one district where two high schools were being transformed into ten new autonomous schools, for example, the district created more design teams than the number of small schools envisioned. Teachers in one school had more support and a better understanding of the small school concept, and so design teams from that school were more successful in creating proposals that incorporated all the elements of small school design. The other school needed more support than it received; it had only one proposal accepted, and this resulted in harsh feelings about the design process.

How are proposals evaluated, and by whom? Whether a conversion effort has more teams than potential school openings or the same number, it needs some process to determine which designs have met the required level. Selection can occur by a team of external reviewers, based on the requirements set out in the RFP, or by allowing the students to "vote with their feet," that is, to select the proposed schools they wish to attend. In one district that used an RFP process, thirteen teams of teachers submitted proposals to start small schools. External reviewers made recommendations on the top seven. Ultimately, all but one school of these seven opened within the range of enrollment that they felt they could serve well. The school that did not receive its minimum necessary enrollment was not opened due to lack of interest, and its prospective students chose among the other six schools.

Opening new small schools enables the district to offer a comprehensive system, a variety of distinct options in which every student has access to every learning environment and in which the environments are designed so that the needs of each student can be met. When choosing which designs to select to form small schools, districts can deliberately ensure that the new schools offer a range of choices and options for students. In the Mapleton Public Schools, for example, the district ensured the creation of schools that follow the principles of Expeditionary Learning and the Coalition of Essential Schools: that there be schools with both art and technology perspectives, schools that support varied learning styles (such as Big Picture High Schools, with schools such as the Met in Providence, Rhode Island, in which students learn through intensive internships and in which each student's learning plan grows out of his or her unique needs, interests, and passions), and schools that provide concurrent college credit (including middle college high schools, where students can attend college classes, and receive college credit that also counts toward a high school diploma).

Small Schools Transition

In this phase, the curricular identity and strategy of the new schools and the policies and procedures that support their design are created. At more or less the same time, the district leadership team finalizes the phase-out plans for the large school's control of the new autonomous schools, and the design team, which has typically expanded to include a core group of the newly approved small school's staff, continues and expands preparations for the opening of new small autonomous schools.

District leadership teams approve decisions on the number of new schools, the timing of their openings, their location and size, the grade levels they will serve when they open, and student access within the district. (These points are all discussed in more detail in Chapter Ten.) They also determine how to best support the students and staff in the large school as it is phased out. In addition, they prepare a final plan for leadership transition, if this has not already been done (see Chapter Eight).

School teams make decisions about their schools' vision and mission, as discussed in Chapter Five, its curricular focus and courses to be offered, as discussed in Chapter Nine, and a whole assortment of policies and practices that constitute a new school. Exhibit 2.2 summarizes the kinds of specific decisions that need to be made in this area.

District Transformation

While it is tempting to focus solely on school-level conversion work, our interviewees emphasized the need for districts to reflect on the policies and procedures they need to change in order to transform their practice to support small autonomous schools instead of or in addition to large comprehensive high schools. For example, we know that one challenge for districts is providing schools with autonomies and changing their own relationships with schools. Districts are involved concurrently in supporting design teams and creating a roll-out plan for the new schools and in self-analysis to create and change their policies and perspective to ones that are supportive of small schools. We discuss these changes in depth in Chapter Three.

In the exploration phase, districts brainstorm the challenges they expect to face and create teams to address those challenges. These teams continue their work, planning for leadership development, teacher professional development, and autonomy and accountability policies—key needs for the district to address before new small schools open. Districts also finalize their plans for assigning students and teachers to schools (discussed in Chapters Eleven and Twelve, respectively).

Implementation

In this phase, some or all of the small autonomous schools open and the district begins to implement new policies and practices. Any remaining design teams are working to open their new schools.

Now that multiple small schools are sharing a building, they finalize the facility decision-making process and structure, which generally includes forming a Building Council (discussed in Chapter Nine). As schools open,

EXHIBIT 2.2.

Creating the Processes, Policies, and Documents That Make Up a New School

Organizational

- Estimated budget
- Fiscal management plan
- Attendance plan

Curriculum, Teaching, and Assessment

- Curricular program overview
- Special education plan
- English language learner plan
- Professional development overview
- Assessment plan
- Data analysis plan

Parents, Students, and Community

- Student recruitment plan
- Student admissions policy
- Registration plan
- Discipline policy
- Parent and student handbook
- Family involvement plan
- Extracurricular and after-school activities plan

Schedule and Calendar

- Daily schedules
- Yearly calendar

Facilities and Physical Plant

- Facilities plan
- Student access and safety
- Health and safety plan

Governance

- School governance structure
- School management plan

Leadership and Staffing

- Staff handbook
- Certificated staffing plan
- Classified staffing plan
- Distributive leadership structure

Logistics for Project Management

- Start-up purchase list
- Application for separate school codes
- College Board code application

Source: *This list is adapted from BayCES.*

other issues arise, such as creating a streamlined communication process with the district, maintaining relationships with community organizations, finding and accessing new resources, and developing the culture and practice of continuous school improvement, as well as continuing support for teachers and administrators to develop their capacity to be successful members of small autonomous schools.

In SeaTac, Washington, Tyee High School—where 49 percent of the student body is eligible for free or reduced-price lunch and where 42 percent of the students are white, 22 percent Asian, 17 percent black, and 16 percent Hispanic—has established a one-year transitional position to help new small autonomous schools in their first year of implementation. This "conversion principal" serves as a liaison between the district and the campus, and as a troubleshooter, responsible for handling all the unseen problems that arise. Having the conversion principal on tap allows the schools to convert more quickly because someone outside the day-to-day responsibilities of running each school handles all the administrative challenges, such as clarifying budgets, shared facilities, and scheduling or transcript problems in the transition year. This frees the directors of the new small schools to focus more explicitly on changing and supporting new instruction practices.

The Small Schools Project (2003a, p. 1) has noted seven "things you can count on happening" in this first year of a new school:

1. *It will be hard to remember that this is a structure in transition, and that your small school is new.*

2. *There will be cross-school tensions.*

3. *There will be ambivalence about leadership.*

4. *Relationships will be closer and therefore more problematic.*

5. *Teaching and learning issues will keep moving down on the agenda.*

6. *We will all feel less effective than before.*

7. *There will be a feeling that the school is really vulnerable.*

The Small Schools Project notes that this first year is full of change, but that the small "schools actually exist . . . and hold untold promise for the students, families, and communities" they serve.

Chapter 3

The District

Supporting Change and Working with Autonomies

FOR CHANGE from large comprehensive high schools to small autonomous schools to sustain itself and improve children's learning experiences, it must be systemic. It occurs in the classroom, the school, and the district. The challenge for the district is in personalizing its support to the particular needs of individual small schools, allowing innovation to flourish in places closest to the learner. The change requires that the district examine and reorganize policies to support the needs of the new and more personalized and flexible schools. As Eric Nadelstern, senior instructional superintendent on the deputy chancellor's staff at the Department of Education in New York City, points out, "You can't design new schools in a school district organized to have exactly the old schools that they're trying to replace." Just as a large school has certain policies and practices that deter personalization, so the district also has practices and policies that serve the needs of large rather than small schools. While comprehensive high schools often need very similar things from their district, small schools—with their own identity, focus, culture, and perspective—have needs very different from one another as well as from their large-school predecessors.

How does a district reorganize itself and its relationship to schools to support this new view of education? How can a district operate as a dynamic, progressive agent of this change? This chapter addresses six main issues:

- The crucial nature of autonomy

- The role of a transformed district

- Examples of how districts are transforming their policies

- Sustaining policies, waivers, and alternatives that support small autonomous schools
- The role of the teachers union
- Extra resources and start-up costs

The Crucial Nature of Autonomy

The key features of successful small schools are that they are mission driven and flexible; schools that are mission driven use their resources to meet their vision, but if the schools are governed from outside themselves, this flexibility is not realized. Karen Hawley-Miles, president of Education Research Strategies and a specialist in resource allocation in urban public school districts, writes that "there is little rationale for restructuring resources without an underlying educational design" (Hawley-Miles & Darling-Hammond, 1997, p. 55). Schools need control over their resources—time, money, people—to serve the unique needs of their students. Smallness and autonomy are features of a school's design that enable the implementation of other principles; they also mutually support one another. Smallness allows for full use of autonomy and autonomy allows for fully building on a school's small size. Combining the work of the Boston Pilot Schools and the Bay Area Coalition for Equitable Schools (BayCES), we regard these six autonomies as vital for small school success:

1. *Budget:* Schools have a lump sum per-pupil budget. Each school may spend its money in the manner that provides the best programs and services to students and their families.

   - The per-pupil budget amount, which is equal to that of other district schools within that grade span, covers instructional materials and other costs of running the school. Ideally, it covers salaries as well, but many districts continue to pay teachers out of a central pool.

   - The district has itemized all central office costs and converted them to a per-pupil equivalent, and now allows schools to choose either to purchase identified discretionary district items and services or to not purchase them and include them in the school's lump sum budget.

2. *School Calendar:* Schools have the freedom to set different school days and calendar years for both students and faculty in accordance with their principles or school reform models. In particular, research supports a correlation between faculty planning time spent on teaching and learning and increased student achievement. Scheduling that allows for summer and school year faculty planning time contributes to a more

unified school community and educational program. Schools use this autonomy for the following purposes:

- Increasing planning and professional development time for faculty
- Increasing learning time for students
- Organizing the school schedule in ways that maximize learning time for students and planning time for faculty

3. *Curriculum and Assessment:* Schools have the freedom to structure their curriculum and assessment practices to best meet students' learning needs. Boston, for example, acknowledges that all Pilot Schools are held accountable to state-required tests, but still gives the schools the flexibility to determine the school-based curriculum and assessment practices that will best prepare students to meet state and district standards.

- Schools have autonomy from local district curriculum and testing requirements—they can choose what content to cover and how to cover it.
- Promotion and graduation requirements are set by the school, not by the district, with an emphasis on competency-based performance assessments.

4. *Governance and Policies:* Schools have the freedom to create their own governance structures that give school staff increased decision-making powers over budget approval, principal selection and firing, and programs and policies, while being mindful of state requirements on school councils. The school's Site Council takes on increased governing responsibilities, including the following:

- Principal selection, supervision, and firing, with final approval by the superintendent in all cases.
- Budget approval.
- Setting of school policies, including schools' promotion, graduation, attendance, and discipline policies.

5. *Staffing:* Schools have the freedom to hire and excess their staff in order to create a unified school community.

- Each school can decide on the staffing pattern that creates the best learning environment for students.
- Each school may hire staff who best fit the needs of the school, regardless of their current status (member of the district or not, although every teacher hired becomes a member of the local teachers union).
- Schools may excess staff (into the district pool) who do not fulfill the needs of the school.

6. *Contiguous and Identifiable Space:* New small autonomous schools should have the freedom to create physical space that is supportive and stimulating for students and teachers. In the case of small schools that share a site, it is particularly important for each to have a sense of place, culture, and purpose for learning. Staff and parents should create a space that helps support the kind of community students, staff, and parents need to get to know one another well. They have autonomy and resources for

   - Remodeling and decorating to establish a distinctive community feel
   - Architectural modifications (within budget) that create spaces conducive to the vision of learning and teaching the school holds

The personalized environment of a small school requires the flexibility to meet students' needs most effectively. Dan French, of the Center for Collaborative Education in Boston, argues, "When you can't identify the staffing patterns that you want to have, the schedule for both faculty and students, when you can't get the autonomy from the district in terms of curriculum, when you have less flexibility in the use of your budget and your governance of your school—all of those things have a huge hindering effect on what you're able to do."

Small school leaders refer to autonomy as vital to a school's ability to "create those conditions in the school which they believe lead to sustained student learning. The use of resource autonomy is directly related to their underlying vision for what a school should be" (Center for Collaborative Education, 2002, p. 36). Small schools create environments where students are well known to their teachers and provide teachers with adequate time to collaborate. Small schools use their autonomy to meet these ideals in a variety of ways, each of which has implications for school practice (Center for Collaborative Education, 2002; Hawley-Miles & Darling-Hammond, 1997).

Examples of how autonomous small schools use their autonomy and flexibility to meet student needs include organizing into even smaller learning units, having smaller class sizes, using looping (where teachers stay with cohorts of students for multiple years), creating student advisories (that is, small groups of students who work with one another and with an adult mentor throughout their time in the school), individualizing the curriculum, and creating smaller student loads for each teacher. Autonomous small schools can use their autonomy to increase the number of staff involved in instruction by having fewer pull-out programs, and by using interns, paraprofessionals, part-time staff, and consultants in the classroom. They use flexible scheduling to allow for extended investigations and explorations, flexible budgeting to put the resources where they best meet the needs of their students, and flexible requirements to craft a curriculum that engages their students on multiple levels.

Autonomous small schools can use creative approaches to staffing to establish the positions that best meet the needs of their students. For example, at Fenway High School in Boston, guidance counselors were performing their traditional roles, giving students information about college, the military, and work. Because of its status as a Pilot School, however, Fenway had the autonomy to change this traditional role. It recognized the need to help students with their emotional and social needs, such as recognizing anorexia, depression, or suicidal gestures. This called for support staff with clinical experience who could run advisories, support teachers, and help students and parents make connections to local clinics and neighborhood services. The school trained other staff to take on the more traditional guidance counselor's roles through the school's advisory program (Center for Collaborative Education, 2002).

The Role of a Transformed District

By providing schools with autonomies and flexibility, the district moves from mandating and monitoring reforms to keeping schools focused on their own unique missions and visions and on improving their instructional practice. The district leads and facilitates policies and practices that enable schools to use their autonomy effectively and make decisions that are central to their vision of instruction. The district must reorganize its whole relationship with schools—its policies and its responsibilities—if it is to provide small schools the conditions and autonomies they need to be successful. We see two new roles.

First, district central offices buffer noninstructional issues, mediate conflicts, and provide those services that are not cost- or time-effective for schools to do on their own or are not part of their core mission. Districts can do work that is easier to do centrally and that takes away from a school's ability to implement its vision.

In one sense, the district becomes a service provider. The district makes many central office costs discretionary, and so becomes more accountable to the needs of each school. Schools can choose to access certain discretionary services or they can instead have the per-pupil funds that the service would cost placed in their lump sum budget. The district needs to work with schools to assess the value of the services on offer and make decisions about which services to staff and fund, which to restructure, and which to phase out because too few schools regard them as valuable enough to buy.

Katrina Scott-George, special assistant to the state adviser in the Oakland Unified School District, which has given significant autonomy to schools, believes that districts need to evaluate their operations: "all of the decisions that we're making about where services are located or who has control over those services to determine who is best positioned to fulfill that role." Schools want to have a say over their lives: the "actual high-leverage decisions and things that the schools need to control as opposed to those that just bog them down in administrative and operational tasks that somebody else could do better."

Too often districts provide poor services to schools and so schools believe that if they could only get control over that activity, they would receive better service. This is not necessarily the case; given equal care and attention, some services really are best provided centrally rather than locally. But it may take the threat of competition to inspire the district to develop an organizational structure responsive enough to support improving teaching and learning.

Edmonton Public Schools in Alberta, Canada, is the best example of a full-service district we have seen. Before their transformation, school staff found that the district's professional development opportunities did not meet their needs. Once the district's professional development office began competing with outside technical assistance agencies to provide support and training for school personnel, it grew more responsive to providing individualized attention to the schools (O'Neil, 1995/1996).

For another example, Edmonton schools complained that the district's building repair services interrupted learning because they insisted on working in regular business hours—that is, during the school day, disrupting the work of the teachers and students. Given a choice to choose their own services, schools decided to employ a repair service that would come in outside school hours. The district's building department responded by changing its practice and offering services during off-hours, which made it attractive enough to win back the schools' business.

Second, the district provides services and support to enable each school to achieve its stated goals and mission. Its staff co-create policies with schools that help schools focus on instruction. For example, districts can manage school accountability practices, helping schools to implement continuous improvement cycles and working with schools to use data effectively to identify and address needs. In the process, districts should model the types of practices expected in schools. As Nadelstern (of the New York City Department of Education) says:

> *If the superintendent gets up once a month in front of a group of principals who are half asleep and hopelessly distracted by the details of the day*

and the challenges of the next day and lectures them mercilessly for two or three or more hours, then those principals are going back into their schools and once a month they're going to have a faculty meeting that looks exactly the same. And what you could expect to see are teachers doing the same in every classroom in that school.

One way to reshape the district is to model the relationships that we want to have in schools. By reorganizing the district with this approach, school and district staff can develop relationships and deep understandings of one another. As Nadelstern says:

If part of the problem in a high school is that it's organized in departmental fashion where nobody's actually responsible for what happens to a kid—the central office is organized exactly the same way. . . . No one person is responsible for what happens in a given school. Everyone has a small piece of every school. . . . And everyone in the organization feels they're responsible for all of the schools but nobody's accountable for any of them. If the idea in a school was to create interdisciplinary teams of teachers who create communities around the needs of manageable numbers of kids, then the district office needs to be organized in exactly the same way. [Districts can create] cross-functional teams responsible and accountable for a small number of schools.

New District Practices

A challenge that has surfaced in conversion work is that few districts undergoing conversion efforts are providing autonomies to their schools. The Year Two evaluation report of the Gates Foundation small schools effort notes that the districts are working on granting new small schools the autonomies with which the districts are comfortable. Typically, this includes curricular and some degree of schedule autonomy. They report that districts are "uncomfortable with major changes in district policies around staffing and budgets to accommodate the needs of the small schools" (American Institutes for Research & SRI International, 2004, p. 95).

Districts that have provided autonomies to their schools have also required more accountability from those schools. BayCES, based in Oakland, California, writes on its Web site: "Autonomies are granted with the expectation of increased accountability on the part of the school to track and demonstrate its progress on raising overall achievement, improving the quality of learning, and showing increased equity of learning outcomes."

In this section, we present three examples of district policies that support the creation and sustainability of small autonomous schools.

Supporting Curriculum and Instruction

Districts can provide leadership for small schools by working with schools to think in depth about the use of resources to support teaching and learning. Mapleton Public Schools, for example, has a single high school in its district. Charlotte Ciancio describes Mapleton's guiding philosophy on supporting small autonomous schools as one that is proactive rather than reactive, that is creating a system that is planful and thinks about what people are trying to accomplish and works from that point, and one that is driven by concerns of instructional practice. Mapleton staff, as in other districts, are deciding which decisions and practices are done best by the district office and which by the school, and how the district can create a framework for schools to have autonomies while staying accountable for their decisions.

Before conversion, when the district made curricular decisions, a district curriculum team would investigate curricula and go through a textbook adoption process. As the district moves to create six autonomous small schools that make their own decisions around curriculum, this policy had to change, and change in a way that focused on supporting instructional practice.

If a school wants to pay for materials with local rather than district money, it does not need to get board approval. If the curriculum is not board approved, and the school wants the district to support it through the acquisition process and use the district textbooks budget, then the school does need to go through a board approval process. Any materials request must include a plan for what the school is going to do with those materials. To get a curriculum approved, the school must address three sets of questions, which Mapleton based on the work of Rick DuFour (DuFour & Eaker, 1998):

> Tell me what it is you're trying to accomplish. Tell me who's going to be part of the decision making that you work through for this. How will you organize yourself to do it, and then what resources do you need?

> What is it that you want kids to know and be able to do? How will you know if they know it? And what will you do if they don't?

> What is it that you're trying to accomplish? What instructional pedagogy will you use? How will you know? What's the assessment? How will you know if kids get it or not? And then what materials do you need to have in order to pull this off?

Budget Autonomy

Staffing makes up the majority of a school's budget, and staffing patterns are typically under the control of the district. Staffing is usually allocated by category (regular education, special education, Title I, bilingual education), combined with a predetermined class size formula for each category and the total number of enrolled students in each category. For example, based on projected enrollment for the coming school year, each traditional school is allotted a certain number of staff and administrative positions using a district's "staffing allocation rules." Everything else (instructional supplies, substitute teachers, stipends, and so on) represents a minute proportion of the school's budget—but nonetheless it is allocated by line item, meaning that funds must be spent within the allocated line item unless prior budget approval is given to move funds to another line item.

Because of these restrictions, most schools lack the flexibility to use their full resources in the effort to maximize student learning. Innovative principals find ways to work around the restrictions, but they often run into bureaucratic obstacles and find themselves distracted from other pressing instructional priorities. The small schools movement, by contrast, relies on local budget control as a way to create the flexible conditions required for innovation. With full budget autonomy, a school can shape its program to the needs of its unique student population and instructional philosophy. Without budget autonomy, small schools cannot make the staffing and scheduling decisions necessary to carry out their missions and visions (Center for Collaborative Education, 2002, p. 13).

For a district to grant schools budget autonomy, it must determine which services are options for schools and then analyze its own budget to determine per-pupil amounts for every line item as well as sub–line items. In Boston, the district determined which central office services were nonessential and gave Pilot Schools—small autonomous schools that were explicitly created to be models of educational innovation in Boston—discretion over whether to purchase those services from the district. (Exhibit 3.1 shows the wording of the relevant provision of the RFP.) If the service was

---

EXHIBIT 3.1

Lump Sum Budgets

All Pilot schools will receive a lump sum budget that is equal to the actual number of students times the average school-based BPS cost per student. The per pupil average will be calculated to include regular education, bilingual education, vocational education, advanced work, and special education students up to and including substantially separate. The actual total funds dispersed to a school will be based on the actual enrollment of students.

Source: *Request for Proposal for 2003–2004 Pilot Schools (Boston Public Schools, 2003).*

not purchased, the per-pupil amount for that service would be added to the school's lump sum budget. In general, Pilot Schools do not purchase these services and consequently these services provide Pilot Schools with significant additional budget flexibility and program support.

In Oakland, schools have "results-based budgeting," which means that they have control over both their general purpose and their categorical funds—but that control is tied to a strategic plan. According to Scott-George, schools have to prepare a plan for student achievement (working with their community and their school Site Council) that describes their priority areas of action, then they must tie the resources to that plan. She says that schools are able to look at both discretionary and general purpose funding sources and say, "These are our priority interventions that we're going to implement and then we will spend the money in this way and then we will look at our data to see did we get the results. The support around how they use their resources is really tied into their support about developing their site plan and then the tracking of their [outcomes]—looking at the data as they prepare the next year's plan to see how they progressed."

Oakland is unique in the country in one facet of results-based budgeting: the actual amount of staff salaries counts against individual schools' budgets, which are calculated on a per-pupil basis. All other districts think in terms of numbers of staff, not cost; that is, they allocate a number of teachers to each school and then pay those teachers whatever they earn, without determining whether one school's staffing is more expensive than another's. Oakland's approach reduces inequities in resources within districts. Because schools that serve high-poverty populations often have teachers with less seniority, their budgets go further under the Oakland model than do the budgets of schools with many veteran educators.

This process also benefits the district, which now has a much more accurate and comprehensive picture of how district funds are allocated. Of course, this examination is liable to find previous inequities in funding.

For example, as noted, when a district pays staffing costs, schools in wealthier areas generally receive more money per pupil because those schools tend to have more experienced staff, people who earn higher salaries than those of the newer teachers who are more likely to be placed in lower-performing schools. Further, in schools where a staff person leaves mid-year, the district still controls the money for the staff position. Often, this position becomes filled by a long-term substitute who costs less than the regular teacher, and the extra money remains in the district office. When a school has control over all its budget, it can decide to put more money into the staffing allocation and hire more staff.

Planning for District Changes

A district needs to envision itself as the focus of change. Districts must recognize that they have to go through transformation simultaneously with the schools if they are to be able to support the schools. Districts can begin this reevaluation and transformation early in the process—as soon as they begin to think about converting large schools to small. In Indianapolis, this is just what is occurring. Although the conversion process began in the fall of 2004, the district leadership had already created work teams to look at specific district needs and policies. Currently, Indianapolis has monthly leadership meetings with both school and district representation. This group has created five workgroups to deal with issues it raised, and members self-selected which team they wanted to work on based on two things—their passion for that particular piece and their desire to ensure that people from similar positions were represented across all five teams. These are the workgroups:

- *District Transformation and Moral Imperative,* which examines practices and policies that need to be changed in order to support the small school movement.

- *Autonomies,* which is looking at creating policy around the areas where schools need to control their own environment and physical and financial resources.

- *Roles and Responsibilities,* which is working on the issues of school leadership and building leadership, and on the elimination of the roles of department chairs, assistant principals, and the principal.

- *Teaching and Learning,* which is looking at the district requirements around standards and instructional frameworks.

- *Equity,* which is focusing on issues of special education, second language learners, and the city's magnet schools, which have unique admission criteria.

These groups included all the principals, the regional directors, the directors of major departments of the central office, the SLC coordinators, and the senior union leadership of each building. The teams meet monthly and are empowered to make recommendations to the district around changes that need to be made to support the work. As we write, forty-nine of the fifty-one recommendations made have been approved by the district.

A New Accountability

Many district leaders worry that giving schools autonomy will lessen their control and ability to ensure that schools are accountable. However, this assumes that the current system does adequately ensure that all district schools are strong. The real question is this: Is there hope that a different accountability structure could be found that would be more likely to ensure that more of a district's schools are strong? Is there reason to believe that this new system could be an improvement?

All schools need to reflect constantly on the quality of their work and the progress and achievements that they make over time. The primary goal of an accountability system should be to help schools improve through critical self-assessment, and it should be linked to appropriate support and intervention for schools that fail to serve their students well and find themselves unable to improve without help.

Fairtest, a nonprofit organization located in Massachusetts that seeks to ensure that evaluation of students, teachers, and schools is fair, open, valid, and educationally beneficial, describes what such an accountability system looks like. Some districts and states, such as Rhode Island, as well as the Boston Pilot Schools and Commonwealth charter schools in Massachusetts, have implemented a school quality review (SQR), similar to the school accreditation process. The SQR model assesses the effectiveness of school practices, including "what students know and are able to do and the quality of opportunities, resources, instruction, and curriculum that are offered to students." The SQR "is one way of providing schools with comprehensive feedback on their practices, while also putting in place a state-wide system of quality control and accountability" (Fairtest, n.d.).

School quality reviews occur every three to five years and can be based on state benchmarks for successful schools. A school creates a school portfolio, collecting reflections and evidence of outcomes and progress in reaching outcomes on performance in each benchmark area.

The district oversees an external team of practitioners and other qualified people who "spend a few days intensively observing students and teachers, interviewing parents, reviewing the portfolio, and collecting evidence to determine whether progress toward meeting the benchmarks was being made. The team also reviews a random sampling of assessments of students who have graduated or been promoted, to determine whether the school's assessments and the students' performances meet the demands of the state benchmarks" (Fairtest, n.d.).

The evaluation concludes with written feedback from the review team, including recommendations for improvement. The school can write a response as well, and both documents, along with the school portfolio, are submitted to the overseeing agency. Schools that do not reach the benchmarks are placed on a one-year follow-up review cycle, with further intervention required if the school still does not make progress.

The Boston School Quality Review Process

The Boston Pilot Schools have increased autonomy with increased accountability through school quality review. The SQR was created by the Pilot School Network, the Center for Collaborative Education, the Annenburg Institute for School Reform, and the Boston Public Schools Office of Research, Assessment, and Evaluation. Pilot Schools are assessed every four years through an elaborate self-study leading to the development of a school portfolio and a school quality review conducted by an external team. This balances the schools' need for autonomy with an outside evaluation effort, which provides new perspectives for the school. It is also a living document that allows the school to "document, reflect upon, and demonstrate its goals, practices and results as they relate to student learning" (Boston Public Schools & Center for Collaborative Education, 2000, p. 4). As Fairtest writes, "A key goal of school quality reviews is to ensure equitable and quality resources and learning opportunities are being provided to all students, and that the school can demonstrate it is working to improve achievement for all students while also closing the achievement gap between low-income and affluent students, and between white students and students of color."

The SQR school portfolio has five sections:

- Vision and Context

- Governance and Budget

- Teaching and Learning—Goals and Results

- Ongoing Professional Support and Improvement

- Family and Community Outreach and External Partnerships

The four- or five-person external review team examines the school portfolio and conducts a three-day visit to the school. The team then completes a School Quality Review Report that is shared with the school and includes recommendations. The school provides a written response to this report outlining how it will implement these recommendations. Both documents are submitted to the superintendent and a joint committee of the district and the teachers union for review. The committee makes a recommendation to the superintendent, who makes a recommendation to the school committee on the future status of the school.

In addition to the school evaluations, the Boston Pilot Schools program includes a provision that the performance of principals and directors should be evaluated every one, two, or three years by their respective governing boards. According to the 2003–2004 RFP:

The cycle of evaluation and the process by which it is conducted should be in writing and approved by the governing board of each school, and be on file with the Superintendent or his designee. The written results of each performance evaluation should be forwarded in a timely manner to the Superintendent or appropriate designee. Based on a review of these evaluations, the Superintendent may choose to initiate further evaluation steps.

This performance evaluation is to be based (at least in part) on the BPS Principles of Effective Leadership, which include competencies such as instructional leadership, quality of parent, student, staff and community relationships, and quality of staff supervision.

Policies, Waivers, and Alternative Provisions

Small school supporters advocate the creation of a system of schooling that questions the traditional one in very basic ways. They are doing so within the context of laws and policies designed to support the typical American high school, and they are pushing for innovative practices that are not supported by the current laws and policies. Districts have two ways of creating policies to support small schools: they can establish *waivers* (alternative provisions to the policy), or they can change the policies that apply to all schools. Waivers allow a way to set up new autonomous small schools but do not create a system of sustainable small schools. Waivers lack sustainability because they themselves are too easy to revoke; they reflect a lack of systemic change in the district and mean that whatever they provide cannot be counted on to continue.

A district serious about conversion needs specific rules for small high schools written into policy. If large schools are to remain in the district, then it will require rules that support their unique needs as well. Absent policy changes, it will be nearly impossible for the small school movement to institutionalize, and it will spend vital resources on the negotiation and renegotiation of waivers rather than committing those resources to teaching and learning. Creating small schools by a "policy of exception" (Darling-Hammond, Ancess, McGregor, & Zuckerman, 2000) will not create the conditions for reinvention to be successful.

Currently, many districts have chosen to use waivers, which can be implemented more easily and quickly than can changes in policy. Of course, this works both ways: it is also easier to take away waivers than it is to change policy. While we agree that written policies should change, however, sometimes the use of waivers is more practical. They provide a way to create the system to support small schools without challenging the traditional structure, and also, in terms of union agreements, without jeopardizing the work status and conditions of teachers at other schools. Another alternative to changing full policy while allowing flexibility from provisions is to create a Memorandum of Understanding. According to Warner-King and Price (2004), MOUs are not as difficult to negotiate as waivers; they provide a trial period for schools to experiment with reforms, and they are easier than waivers to revise and tinker with. However, it is key that successful innovations be protected by policy.

The Role of the Teachers Union

Union contracts and collective bargaining agreements govern much of what happens in the day-to-day life of schools: salary schedules, work hours, planning time, transfer and assignment policies, hiring, and grievance procedures, among other things. Much like district policies, collective bargaining agreements have also been written with large comprehensive schools in mind, and often preclude the agreements needed to support work in small schools. Many small school practices can run counter to a typical collective bargaining agreement.

For example, in small schools, teachers wear many hats: student adviser, core academic teacher, elective teacher. They spend time collaborating with other teachers to create interdisciplinary curricula, and they have more say in the governance of the school than do most of their counterparts in large schools. Teachers also may have uncompensated demands placed on them, or spend uncompensated time in the planning and design of new schools.

We have found a wide range of union responses to large school conversions, including many unions that have been active supporters of the conversion process out of a belief that conversion can significantly improve working conditions for teachers. Some unions, such as New York City's United Federation of Teachers, accept an arrangement that, if a certain percentage of teachers within a school agree, school staff can select new hires without regard to seniority rights. The conversion effort needs to pay attention and spend the time necessary to work with the union to address these complex issues.

For example, the collective bargaining agreement typically applies to every school in a district. If some but not all schools are converting, districts and unions may be reluctant to grant modifications for fear that they will set a precedent for all schools in the district. The best short-term solution may be a waiver or alternative provision, rather than challenging the existing contract, but with an understanding that the new contract will be able to support both small and large schools, if necessary. Only if the waivers or alternative provisions are written into policy are small schools assured that their practices are institutionalized. Further, various efforts have implemented provisions for working with the union to formalize leadership positions, to provide some stipend for uncompensated time, or to provide alternative supports that benefit the working conditions of teachers and their relationship with students (such as additional preparation periods) or paid leave.

According to Warner-King and Price (2004, pp. 28–29), unions offer three particularly useful roles in supporting small schools:

- Perspective. *Unions can offer perspective on the impacts of small school reform efforts on all teachers district-wide, not just teachers at small schools. This perspective can help small schools anticipate and respond to potential objections from other teachers (e.g., concerns about reallocating planning time, increasing the number of preparation periods, etc.).*

- Expertise. *Unions have experience and expertise in areas such as collaboration, shared decision-making, communication, public relations, budgeting, organizational mediation, and educational issues such as No Child Left Behind (NCLB).*

- Resources. *Unions often have full-time staff members available to assist teachers and schools with training and staff development, data collection, research analysis, and public relations.*

Exhibit 3.2 provides an illustration of the provisions involved in working out a union agreement.

Extra Resources and Start-Up Costs

A district does have significant resources at its disposal—even if they may be difficult to identify at first glance. For example, all districts provide some professional development time. Districts can also work with the union to free up more time for teachers, such as by slightly modifying their school calendar and schedule. Our goal here is to help districts be more planful in their use and allocation of resources in the course of a conversion effort, whether or not they find themselves able to line up extra resources from outside.

Some conversion teams that we spoke with proceeded with very little external money; they were able to get the job done by making the most of their current resources. Others have found extra resources through public grants such as the Department of Education's Small Learning Communities

---

EXHIBIT 3.2

Example of Union–Autonomous Schools Policy: Teacher Salaries and Work Conditions

---

Teachers, paraprofessionals, nurses, guidance counselors, substitutes, and all other employees at Pilot Schools who fall under the jurisdiction of the BTU contract will be members of the appropriate BTU bargaining unit.

These employees shall accrue seniority in the system and shall receive, at a minimum, the salary and benefits established in the BTU contract.

Employees in Pilot Schools will be required to work the full day/work year as prescribed in the terms of the individual Pilot Schools proposal. Further they shall be required to perform and work in accordance with the terms of the individual Pilot School proposal. Nothing in the Agreement shall prevent Pilot School governing bodies from making changes to their programs and schedules during the year.

Employees shall work in Pilot Schools on a voluntary basis and may excess themselves at the end of the school year. No BTU member may be laid off as a result of the existence of Pilot Schools.

Pilot School contracts with employees must stipulate the salary, benefits, and terms of employment being offered to the prospective employee and must be consistent with the above provisions.

Source: *Request for Proposal for 2003–2004 Pilot Schools (Boston Public Schools, 2003).*

---

program (for fiscal year 2004, the award for eligible schools ranged from $650,000 to $1,175,000 depending on the size of the school), as well as from private foundations, most notably the Bill & Melinda Gates Foundation, which has spearheaded small autonomous school initiatives across the country. Conversion teams have also supplemented their resources by working with local foundations and organizations. Indeed, such relationships are so useful that the Ohio-based KnowledgeWorks Foundation—which is supporting an extensive small schools and conversion initiative in its state—requires that conversion efforts partner with a local community organization that will provide resources and support.

Conversion is a significant change process. During the different conversion phases, the team will face issues involving communication, community engagement, research, design, policy development, and troubleshooting, as well as core professional development and capacity-building tasks that initiatives must attend to (as we describe in more detail in Appendix E), all of which they will need to fund—either with existing resources or with resources newly secured for the purpose. Some teams need to refurbish an existing school building; others have outlays for hothousing (locating new schools in other buildings). Conversion initiatives have found a number of ways to line up the necessary resources. New supplemental funds (beyond what is available within the district or local budget) have primarily been used for professional development to build staff capacity in skills related to small schools and their development, or to cover stipends and hire additional personnel during planning, transition, and initial small schools implementation.

As we discuss in Chapter Six, conversion teams must assess what level of support teachers may need in developing skills to be effective in the instructional strategies and collaborative professional community essential to small schools. This will shape whether schools may access existing professional development funds or need to find additional resources for capacity building by shifting funds or securing outside grants. Funds for professional development have been used to pay for technical assistance and training as well for teacher stipends and for substitutes to cover release time.

Stipends have also been used to compensate staff for time spent on new school design and the creation of policies and practices that are part of opening new schools. Some conversion teams have been able to provide significant release time for staff professional development or design work. Some initiatives have chosen to bring on temporary personnel. During the design phase, typical personnel costs include hiring a headmaster or community engagement coordinator. As new schools open, districts may need to fund an extra position, such as Tyee High School's one-year transitional conversion principal, described in Chapter Two, to handle the many tasks that occur during the transition and to ensure a smoother transition.

Concluding Thoughts

Creating schools for the Information Age requires more than just changing schools; the policies and procedures that govern them must change to support them. Small schools have different needs from larger ones—and from one another; educators involved in conversion and small schools are finding that the policies that support large comprehensive high schools—the very schools we are saying do not meet the needs of our students—will not allow small schools to flourish. If districts keep doing what they have been doing and hope for different results from what they have been getting, they will be frustrated. For small schools to survive and thrive, a different relationship between schools and the district is necessary. New systemic policies that create flexibility and new models of accountability within a bureaucratic system are required.

Chapter 4

Stakeholder Engagement

IT IS A STRAIGHTFORWARD principle that the people who are affected by a decision will naturally want to be involved in that decision. If administrators or teachers are the only stakeholders at the table, then the plan they create has a significant chance of not taking into account what students, district staff, or community members need. It is likely to upset or alienate those who were left out. A broad range of stakeholders—not only teachers and school site administrators, but also parents, district staff, community members, and business leaders, in addition to students—are essential. Their sense of ownership of the change is needed for the short- and long-term success of the initiative.

In this chapter, we discuss the stakeholders in depth, set up a framework for thinking about the process of engagement, and provide examples of how some efforts have done so. We share findings and strategies for cultivating community, parent, and student involvement in and ownership of the conversion process. The strategies address how, in practice, conversion efforts can facilitate ownership and go beyond buy-in. Engagement lays the foundation for the conversion and for stakeholders' contributions to the ongoing work of small schools.

Engage Stakeholders Early and Often

Perspectives on the community role in conversion leadership have notably shifted from early conversion initiatives (those started prior to 2002) to later efforts. Many early conversion efforts did not involve the community, and as a result they met considerable resistance and stalled in creating autonomous schools, at best creating small learning communities instead.

Among later efforts almost all include parents; some also include students on new school design teams, but the extent to which they are kept involved varies widely. Only one effort we spoke with trains students and parents to be leaders; three initiatives require that new schools partner with an existing community organization that provides leadership on the design team and support for the newly created school, and one effort requires that a community organization run multiple public forums about the nature of education and feed community views back into the design process.

The Harwood Institute of Public Innovation, a Bethesda, Maryland–based organization dedicated to being a catalyst for change, provides five ideas to guide community engagement:

- Pursue civic engagement, not public input.

- Engage people as citizens, not consumers.

- Discover voices, not simply demographics.

- Seek common ground, not consensus.

- Provide knowledge, not more information.

For a detailed look at the Harwood Institute's principles of civic engagement, which will be useful to anyone engaged in a small schools conversion effort, see Appendix F.

The Harwood Institute's Path of Public Knowledge (see Figure 4.1) illustrates a way to engage stakeholders up front. The Harwood staff believe that conversations about change must start from people's *values, beliefs, and aspirations.* When conversations begin by discussing values and aspirations, stakeholders can absorb a wide range of perspectives, see that they have more common ground than differences, and develop a common understanding and shared vision. The discussion process also allows valuable information, perspectives, and resources to be shared and ongoing relationships of support and collaboration to be established. Stakeholders can then identify and discuss the *trade-offs* inherent in that vision, because they have become clearer about what they most value. After these conversations occur, stakeholders can make decisions on *policy choices.* As can be seen from the figure, the closer one comes to making decisions on policy options, the fewer options are presented.

By being part of the process from the beginning, stakeholders see and understand the trade-offs that created the final choices. Too often, stakeholders are brought into the process when the decision has come down to two options—in this case, the decision to convert or not. Such a narrow choice makes it inevitable that the process must have winners and losers, and it evokes resistance. When stakeholders face policies they have not

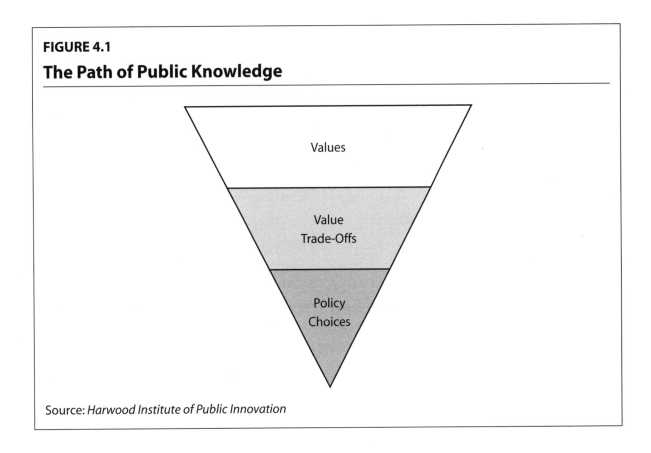

FIGURE 4.1

The Path of Public Knowledge

Values

Value
Trade-Offs

Policy
Choices

Source: *Harwood Institute of Public Innovation*

helped to create and do not understand they are more likely to raise questions and to try to slow or stop the change process.

For example, Shaw High School in East Cleveland, Ohio, which enrolls more than twelve hundred students, 40 percent of whom are ninth graders and almost 100 percent are African American, had very strong vocational programs—programs that school leaders wanted to eliminate as they moved to create new autonomous small schools. When this plan was brought to the community, the community was greatly upset. The career training was important, school leaders were informed, in that it trained students for jobs that provided funds that they then used to pay for higher education. Ultimately, the vocational programs were integrated in a way that kept to the goals of the school designs. In conversion, as with other major change endeavors, leaders are effective when they understand the perspectives, capacities, values, needs, hopes, and fears of the people who are important to the success of their endeavor.

Engaging stakeholders early, often, and broadly provides four benefits:

First, bringing stakeholders into the process from the beginning creates a partnership rather than a sense that change is being imposed from the outside or from the top down.

Second, through engagement efforts, stakeholders can learn about conversion and have their questions addressed. School leaders found that identifying issues that people fear, addressing them up front, and putting in structures and systems that deal concretely with those concerns where appropriate was a tremendous benefit. In Exhibit 4.1, we list the matters stakeholders most often want to address.

EXHIBIT 4.1

Typical Stakeholder Questions

Teachers ask:

- What does this mean for my job?
- How does this change my working conditions?
- What do I teach?
- Who do I teach?
- Do I get to keep my job?
- What kind of support do I get in this change?
- What role do I play in making this decision?
- How can I teach advisories?
- How can I teach heterogeneous groupings of students?

Parents ask:

- What does this mean for my child?
- Will my child still have AP classes? A college prep education? Will my child be able to participate in sports, band, or choir?
- Will this limit my child's choice of classes and electives?
- Does it affect college entrance or career choice?
- What role do I play in making this decision?

Students ask:

- What about my friends—what if they are in another school?
- How do I get to choose my school?
- What if I don't get my first preference?
- What if I don't like any of the choices?
- What does this mean for my relationships with teachers?
- What are the answers to most of the parents' questions?

Administrators and district staff ask:

- How can we afford start-up costs?

- What extra resources are required?

- How do we grant schools' autonomies and then make best use of them?

- What policies must we change to support small schools?

Others may have questions of their own:

- School board

- Teachers union

- Community members

- Businesses and public sector organizations

Third, by engaging with one another, school staff, students, parents, and community members can share their concerns of aspirations for their schools and have them incorporated into school designs.

Fourth, conversations with stakeholders lay the groundwork for community support of the small autonomous schools that are created. Engagement with the community is an integral part of both the change process *and* the ongoing work of a small school. The goals of engagement in change will differ somewhat from the goals that guide the ongoing work of a school, but the way engagement occurs in conversion ideally sets the pattern for how such relationships will be sustained. The conversion process is a way to engage community groups more deeply in the business of schooling, as well as highlighting the relationship between the schools and the community, creating lasting ties and partnerships, and developing resources for both the school and the community to draw on.

Educators we spoke with underscored that an important task for conversion initiatives is to reframe and restructure the nature and the purpose of the relationships among members of a school community. School reform and organizational change research suggests that for a conversion to be successful in the long run, all those involved in intentionally created small schools must be aligned around the new mission of educating all students for college readiness and around the practices that enable this mission to succeed. Early reports and interviews indicate that for conversion to small schools to achieve such alignment, the critical task of the conversion process is to take everyone who works within the school community through a paradigm shift. All must set aside the mission and practices that undergirded the large comprehensive high school and move toward the new vision of small schools. When all members of the school community—students, teachers, parents, administrators, and nonprofit or business partners—come to a shared understanding on the ultimate purpose of schooling, then they can align their attitudes and behavior to support the mission and ensure that students succeed.

Go Beyond Buy-In: Stakeholder Ownership

Though many educators spoke of needing buy-in from stakeholders, in light of our own and other research on school changes, buy-in is perhaps not sufficient to achieve conversion objectives. People with a strong sense of personal direction and commitment can join together to create a powerful synergy to work toward and achieve a goal they truly want (Senge, 1990). This synergy and commitment requires more than the mild acquiescence generally implied by the term *buy-in*. Building a synergy of individual efforts is a basic principle of powerful organizations and effective organizational change. Authentic commitment to a shared goal of enabling all students to be ready for college is a driver for undergoing the challenging work of conversion. If a commitment and common vision are not established for difficult or controversial reforms, initiatives usually secure buy-in or at minimum compliance with reforms from those involved—which can fall short of producing the transformation and results needed for the historical shift in mission and structure entailed in conversion.

For example, the technology of teaching in effective small schools is based on a teacher's intrinsic commitment to, ownership of, and responsibility for outcomes of learning for each and every student. The move to small schools requires that teachers transform their pedagogical practice, using approaches such as differentiating instruction within classrooms, which is pivotal to enabling all students to achieve at the highest levels. Teachers must make endless decisions about who their students are and what they need (learning styles, skill levels, best differentiated teaching strategy) and find ways to adapt their curriculum to respond to individual and class dynamics. Teachers' commitment to do whatever it takes to meet the vision for teaching, learning, and achievement in a small school is what will ultimately produce authentic change. No amount of leadership by a principal, standardization of curriculum and assessment, or external demands or pressures can substitute for teachers' and students' ownership of the learning experience. This is a dramatic shift from what has been possible and common given the limitations in a traditional comprehensive high school. Such change cannot be mandated.

If teachers only go along with the changes, the change is unlikely to be as transformative or deep as needed and is less likely to be sustained or fully integrated over time. In a small school, one teacher can have a significant impact on the emerging culture. For example, effective small schools require teacher collaboration. A teacher who is only compliant with the change may continue to try to work in isolation, thereby undermining the collaborative inquiry important to the school's overall success—and no amount of individual talent and in-class effectiveness will counterbalance the resulting injury to the fabric of the small school.

Senge (1990) provides a framework for understanding the difference in levels of commitment and the implication of those differences for being able to harness and direct the energy of a school community toward a common goal. As we conceive it, *ownership* means that people are committed enough to the vision to actively, creatively address problems, create programs, design strategies, and build structures to make vision happen even though people will have different opinions about the particular structures or strategies. Ownership implies commitment to work out these differences in the name of moving forward to accomplish the vision. This is the stance needed for both conversions and small schools to accomplish their mission. Senge contrasts ownership with other commitment levels in which people will do whatever can be done within the spirit of the law, and with compliance, in which people on the whole see the benefits of the vision and do what's expected and no more, and with noncompliance ("I won't do it, and you can't make me") and apathy, in which people have no interest and no energy.

Examples of Community, Parent, and Student Involvement

In this section we present examples and strategies for how conversion efforts have cultivated community, parent, and student involvement in and ownership of the conversion process.

Community Involvement

KnowledgeWorks in Ohio, BayCES in California, and the New York City Public Schools have all engaged community organizations to great effect and support of the change process. Community-based organizations have served as catalysts and true partners in the reform. Community organizations are rarely very involved in school reform, although typically not from lack of interest. Instead, there have been challenges of building alliances and communicating across language or other barriers. Community organizations have helped support the small school movement in a number of ways:

- Placing political pressure on city and school leadership and teacher unions to support the change

- Communicating information and engaging members of the community in discussions about schools and education

- Working collaboratively and in partnerships with conversion design teams and new schools to provide design support, in-kind and donated resources, or professional support

Political Pressure

Oakland Community Organizations (OCO) is a faith-based collaborative representing more than thirty thousand members from thirty-five Oakland churches and other community organizations. OCO was concerned about the quality of education for Oakland's children. It began working to organize parents and community members in response to low-performing, overcrowded, unsafe schools. OCO sought the educational expertise of BayCES and together formed an alliance with the Oakland Unified School District. This alliance helped spark educational transformation in the district. OCO and BayCES developed a vision of what education could be like for all of Oakland's children centered around small, autonomous, and personalized schools. Pressure from OCO and other groups prompted the Oakland School Board to pass the Small Schools Policy unanimously in May 2000. Since that time, BayCES has provided assistance to the district, which has successfully converted two large comprehensive high schools into small autonomous schools. This partnership has sustained the movement to create and sustain small autonomous schools in Oakland through a number of complex challenges, including a financial and political crisis and a state takeover of the district.

Communicating with and Engaging Community in Dialogue

KnowledgeWorks, in conjunction with an approach developed by the Harwood Institute, places a community-based organization (CBO) at the center of their conversion plan. KnowledgeWorks requires that all schools exploring conversions establish a partnership with a CBO—what the Harwood Institute calls a "Center of Strength." The Center of Strength has multiple responsibilities in both the conversion process and in the functioning of the new small schools. To support this community approach, KnowledgeWorks makes an additional grant to a local nonprofit entity that is held in esteem or regard within that community.

In East Cleveland, Ohio, the Greater Cleveland Regional Transit Authority (GCRTA) became the Center of Strength for Shaw High School.

Annie Lott, then district director of the Hayden Garage, organized almost twenty community meetings, held at churches, the local library, the YWCA, and an adult training and education center (but none at the school itself) on weeknights, Saturday mornings, and Sunday afternoons. Using the *Public Engagement and Small Schools Conversation Guide* (2002), published by the Harwood Institute, Lott and her colleagues listened to the community's hopes for education. They reviewed their effectiveness at facilitating meetings, examined the feedback they received, and summarized the information based on the questions asked. They emerged with a list of ten ideas that were held in common, such as higher levels of learning, teachers who can individualize lessons for the unique needs of the community, increased safety, and having schools that were receptive to them and that could be a center of the community. The community also discussed what they liked about the current school, such as the band and the school's vocational programs. The GCRTA placed ads in the free weekly papers thanking the community for its support and describing these ten key beliefs they heard from the community.

The GCRTA listened to the community and relayed the information about what the community wanted from high school education back to the building, which tried to incorporate these ideas. Shaw High School opened as five small autonomous schools in the fall of 2004, and the schools that share the building have created a common Parent Welcome Center to be more receptive to parents who come to the school. They also incorporated the old vocational programs—which the school staff had intended to eliminate—into the new schools. Still at the start of their conversion process, the schools are working on many other ideas, such as using the schools after-hours to create an adult training program. The GCRTA is continuing its engagement with the community, with several planned meetings to go back to the community to revisit the common beliefs and how the schools can implement them effectively.

Partnerships and Collaboration

The Center of Strength has other responsibilities in the design envisioned by KnowledgeWorks and the Harwood Institute. It has one representative on the school's design team during the early phases; once the school breaks down into smaller schools, the Center of Strength provides support to each of them.

KnowledgeWorks involves the community in other ways as well. As part of the schoolwide self-analysis, schools rate themselves based on perspectives of stakeholders; teachers, parents, students, and the community. Further, after being awarded a conversion grant, a school is required to find a community partner—not the Center of Strength—who will provide $100 per student for the high school.

Annie Lott saw the GCRTA's role as the Center of Strength as mutually beneficial to both groups. The GCRTA had declining ridership, noticed that many applicants applying for jobs were unprepared and unqualified, and needed new bus mechanics to replace a large cohort nearing retirement. In assuming the Center role, the GCRTA could give back to the community, keep the community apprised of its services and problems, and develop new leaders in its own organization. GCRTA employees served on the design teams for each of the new schools. The school that ultimately became the School of Entrepreneurship, Finance, and Transportation built on the school's mechanical program, which had been in danger of being eliminated. The GCRTA liaison was very useful in helping the school develop this program—and in the process created a pathway to provide students with the skills needed to become bus mechanics.

In the Bronx the New York City district made a concerted effort to connect each of its new small schools with a CBO or other organization that participates in the community. The community partner has joint responsibility for the development of the proposal and ongoing assessment of the school, and shares in the development and the running of the school as well. As Eric Nadelstern says:

> We said to [the CBOs] initially that either they could continue to try to define themselves as coming in after school and undoing the damage that we do from 9:00 to 3:00 or they could really roll up their sleeves and join us in rethinking what happens to kids from 9:00 to 5:00. Those that came forward were very sincere and genuine in their effort to help us rethink school in a way that not only redefined those schools but also redefined themselves as organizations.

Peter Steinberg concurs:

> We have learned that it is incredibly important to engage the full community in this process and that means students, parents, community organizations, and cultural organizations. And to bring them in from the very beginning and to work with them and teachers and possible administrators for schools and to free people up to use their imagination and their creativity and their commitment to create the kind of schools that they have never been allowed to even dream of, the kind of schools to which they can have some kind of serious commitment, and then to provide them with the support that is necessary for them to gain an understanding of nontraditional means of engaging young people and of challenging young people in schools so that small schools can be created which are,

in fact, going to be effective small schools. . . . [Community organizations] bring a very different perspective as well as additional resources to these schools. I think that you have to work with existing populations but to bring them over a period of time to a consciousness that there are other ways of doing things—and to allow them to see the reality of that.

For example, East Side House Settlement is the founder and community partner of Mott Haven Preparatory High School. It shares its technology staff and has co-located its youth leadership staff at the high school to serve the freshmen and sophomores, although they also serve juniors and seniors from other high schools. Staff from the school and the community organization meet together and share expertise. Staff at East Side have social work expertise that has enabled them to work with Mott Haven staff in conducting student advisories, and they are steeped in the culture and community of the South Bronx. For its part, East Side House Settlement is benefiting from the pedagogical expertise of the school staff, which has translated to improvements in the after-school programs that its people run in other schools.

Student and Parent Involvement

Indianapolis began its conversion process by signing into agreement a Memorandum of Understanding for creating small schools in October 2003. The Indianapolis school district includes five large comprehensive schools, ranging in enrollment from fifteen hundred to twenty-two hundred students, 63 percent of whom are African American, 30 percent white, and 68 percent eligible for free or reduced-price lunch. In February 2004 each of the five high schools began an official exploration period, supported by grant money that lasted until the end of the year, at which point the district began the process of supporting design teams in creating small autonomous schools.

From the beginning of this process, students and parents have had a central voice. Megan Howey, director of the Vista Service Learning Demonstration Project, which is sponsored by the Harmony Education Center in Bloomington, Indiana, has created five ways to involve parents and students, with plans to develop these ideas further.

- City leaders, community members, and school leaders were invited to a citywide grant kickoff in fall 2003. Students from each of the five high schools facilitated and added to small group dinner conversations about high schools, small high schools, and small learning communities.

- Thirty students from each of the five schools were supported in school-based Youth Forums, leading to a Youth Congress at which students discussed what their ideal school would look like and what students, teachers, and parents can do to help create a school environment that will help everyone learn.

- At least one student has joined each of the exploration teams. On these teams, students have surveyed their peers to bring back student ideas to the exploration team or have conducted a student profile activity in which students shared "what teachers need to know about me to teach me well."

- One hundred students and parents attended a summer Leadership Institute to develop the skills to engage in conversations about education generally and conversion specifically. This Institute overlapped with school staff critical friends group training (discussed in Chapter Six), and the two groups came together for conversation.

- Almost a hundred parents and thirty students attended a Parent Congress, funded by the district and a parent leadership organization in Indiana called the Partnership Center. The aim of that event was to educate parents about the small school process and help them understand how they can talk with teachers and how they can ask the right questions. Students, parents, and teachers spoke together about what parent involvement can look like and how parent involvement in the small school process deepens the work.

Parents

Historically, parent involvement in high school has been low, and this is particularly true of parents of low-income students or students of color. Creating new small schools can break this cycle through the formal inclusion of parents on the design team as well as seeking out the views of these parents in more informal circumstances.

BayCES has included parent and student voices as members of the design team to great impact. Fremont High School, an Oakland school with more than eighteen hundred students (48 percent Hispanic, 30 percent African American, and 19 percent Asian, with 62 percent eligible for free or reduced-price lunch), was reborn as the Fremont Educational Complex: five new small autonomous schools. Maureen Benson, principal of Youth Empowerment School (YES), which opened with a ninth grade at the Fremont Educational Complex, believes that involving parents in the design team leads to three dramatic benefits for her school: parents had insights that shaped the design of the school, and the school built relationships with parents even before the new small school opened, beginning the process of institutionalizing the mutually supportive relationship between the school and the parents. "[Parents on the design team] really provided a lens that was essential for us in the continuous development of our government and in community expectations of what we wanted to see in the classrooms."

Benson continues to work with parent liaisons to connect with parents, and holds town hall meetings for parents to discuss their concerns. She says:

> *The town hall meetings are not just information sessions but dialogues and debates about the issues, about what we want to see change, and how can we address them. People are really engaging and feel like their voices are heard. It's this continuous cycle where parents are having input and they're seeing response to it. This coupled with the fact that I took that first step to build a relationship with them before their kid even started seems to have had pretty good success. . . .*
>
> *Trust your parents. I've had parents articulate better than I ever could what a teacher could do to improve or what structural things could happen in the school to enhance the community. They have higher stakes than we all do in it. So really, truly trusting in them and giving them the opportunity to constructively support the school is awesome and yields better results and better relationships.*

For example, parents had concerns about the quality of teaching and the level of challenge their children received in YES's first year, and in response Benson held a training and information session:

> *We had thirty or forty people [of a school of a hundred students] show up. I just asked them, "What would you want to ask a teacher? What characteristics are you looking for if you do a classroom observation?" The rubrics and the questions that they came up with—you could sell it. They were so good. I mean they were incredible interview questions. Really thought-provoking interview questions that would indicate immediately whether a teacher was adequate. The things that they're looking for in the classroom observations—the district couldn't have written a better tool.*

Life Academy in Oakland, the first new school to emerge from an academy at Fremont High School, opened in 2001 with 250 students, Grades 9–12. With the support of OCO, Laura Flaxman, founding principal of the school, was able to have representatives from the school go door-to-door in the school's neighborhood to talk with parents. Reaching out to parents typically disempowered by schools, as Life Academy and YES did, is necessary to disrupt this cycle.

Students

Students were essential elements in the creation of Life Academy. A design team consisting of students, parents, teachers, and administrators pioneered designing and opening the first small autonomous school created in Oakland.

Involving students in the design team had three positive impacts on the development of the school. First, Flaxman says, "We had these incredible student leaders who were twelfth graders who had been tremendously involved in starting the schools. They had hired the teachers, they had designed the student agreements, they had designed the staff agreements. We did those together so that people had an input on each other's [work]. They designed the student government and served on it. The level of ownership in the school was unbelievable."

Second, this level of ownership contributed to an increased belief in small schools. The students on the design team talked with their friends about the school, and built more buy-in and interest from the student community before the conversion occurred. Third, when the school opened, students were more likely to continue to make suggestions and work to improve their school community.

Students believed they benefited greatly from being members of the design team. One said, "I learned a lot about how the school system is being run. At one point I actually wanted to . . . make changes in school or either become a teacher, a counselor in school, or a person in the government that deals with school stuff, like a school board member. And I learned how to be outspoken, how to get my thoughts across" (Flaxman, 2004, p. 5).

Concluding Thoughts

The creation of small schools requires a cultural shift in the way that everyone—students, teachers, and community members—view what schools do, what students need to know, how they really learn, and how they should be taught. It requires a shift in how stakeholders interact to create a distinct new space and culture at the school. This requires building a vision together—and that provides the opportunity to set a context for the launch of new schools. We hope that seeing the multiple places that community members and organizations can and have affected the educational system for the better will help conversion efforts to engage with the community in more productive and authentic ways, to make a new structure, culture, and instructional approach that works for young people. Doing so changes the conversation and enhances not only the sustainability of the reform but its effectiveness as well.

Part 2

Founding Autonomous, Interconnected Schools

Chapter 5
School Vision

SCHOOL FOR SOCIAL JUSTICE. Mandela Academy. The Academy of Journalism and Communication. School for Physical Science. Excel Academy. The School for the Performing Arts. Human Kinetics and Wellness School.

These are the names of just a few of the hundreds of new schools that have been created as part of the movement to convert large comprehensive high schools to small autonomous schools. Their variety and profusion reflect the emergence of schools designed *not* to be comprehensive. Instead, such schools, in their effort to integrate curriculum and learning, often narrow their focus based on the maxim, "less is more." Regardless of its focus, each school seeks to develop a coherent educational vision geared to offering students an integrated and engaging learning experience. These schools concentrate on a specific topic of interest or social value, ground learning in student internships or apprenticeships with outside organizations or professionals, rely on project-based pedagogies, or seek to provide skills particularly suited to the current economy.

School Vision That Supports Mastery for All

Developing a clear statement of the vision of the new school is one of the most critical tasks a school undertakes. A vision statement is a powerful tool in guiding the actions of a group along a common path. The school identity, vision, or theme—whatever you wish to call it—is the vehicle to implement the school's vision of teaching and learning. For conversion efforts that need to shift their practices, it is particularly important to develop a vision focused on effective teaching and learning that supports all students. A school's vision ultimately drives its unique design, including its structure, culture, and instructional approach. Based on lessons learned from conversions to date, here are five questions to keep in mind when deciding on a school vision and curricular identity:

- *Engagement:* How can we devise curriculum and instruction that will engage our students?

- *High expectations:* How can we develop a distinct new culture where the adults at the school hold high expectations for all our students?

- *Community resources:* How can we best take advantage of resources in our community, including museums, theaters, nonprofit groups, local government, businesses, and the like?

- *Thematic content:* How can a focus on certain areas of human learning engage students to deepen their mastery of content and core skills? In what ways will we integrate this focus into our school practice and design?

- *Instructional style:* What do we believe teaching needs to look like at this school? How will teachers and students interact? How will we include and support all students?

Peter Steinberg, director of the Bronx New Century High Schools, says:

[Vision is] something that schools have to be very careful of and very conscious of. Even if they go to a Health Academy or an Academy of Law, the kids are not going come out of school being doctors or lawyers. They should come of these schools being thoughtful people who have— in our terminology—developed habits of mind and work. This will make them effective wherever they go and whatever they do. To succeed, there needs to be an understanding that these habits of mind and work are the deeper goals—and that the themes are simply a means to engage kids.

One of the great strengths of small schools—as we see it—is their ability to integrate their curricular focus throughout the school, to use it as a lens through which students explore their world and develop skills, deepen their knowledge, and learn to direct their own learning. The key for a school is to develop a tool that helps the students study and understand a range of content. This could, for example, involve looking at core classes and electives of secondary study from the perspective or in the context of social justice, technological development, or global issues.

George York is principal of Bronx High School for the Visual Arts, which at the time of our interviews was one of five small autonomous schools that resided in the same building as Columbus High School, a large comprehensive school. He describes his school (which opened with a class of eighty-five ninth graders in fall 2002) and its focus on the arts in these terms:

"Since we are an arts school, arts are integral not only as a separate discipline but also as they integrate into the other areas. Teachers from all disciplines understand that they are going to use the arts to facilitate learning and for collaborative work." Schools with a strong intellectual vision like the Bronx High School for the Visual Arts help students attain a set of skills, build content knowledge, develop a repertoire of approaches to problems and challenges, and learn how to learn.

School Identity Is More Than a Theme

Though our reading of the small school literature and our interviews with educators from high-functioning small schools leads us to wholeheartedly support the notion of an instructional focus, we also sound a cautionary note. We have encountered a number of examples in which focus on developing a school's theme has seemed to distract from attention to the deeper purpose of schooling—that students will gain skills and learn to think deeply and flexibly about a wide variety of issues. The theme might provide the school with an intriguing name, but it does not ensure intellectual depth or vitality, nor does it automatically address issues of equity.

Holli Hanson, a member of the Small School Project Coach Collective in Seattle, Washington, shared with us some of her reservations about "theme schools." According to Hanson, themes provide an easy box for students and teachers to think in, but "there are some advantages of people really having to explore the notion of what they believe about powerful teaching and learning, what is that going to look like, before considering whether they are going to have a theme or not. I think people can hide behind the theme." For example, a design team may be drawn to the idea of starting a school for the arts because of a potential partnership with a local museum. The design team may not, however, be fully invested in an integrated arts approach—and so they stick with their old curriculum, with an arts add-on; they don't create a new curriculum through which students use arts as a lens to understand and learn about math, science, and other subjects. The theme of the school is a kind of window dressing; it is potentially false advertising to parents and students as to what young people will experience in the classroom.

Examples of School Visions

Small schools are being created with a rich range of visions and curricular approaches, often involving a broad array of stakeholders in exciting ways.

When South Shore High School in Chicago, a large comprehensive high school of approximately eleven hundred students (99 percent African American, 61 percent eligible for free or reduced-price lunch), began to think about converting, Bill Gerstein, then an assistant principal, was part of a team that developed Entrepreneurship High School, which opened in the fall of 2001 with more than a hundred African American ninth graders. Gerstein's design team's choice for school vision and curricular identity was linked to an assessment of what would motivate students in the school and help them develop skills of benefit to themselves and their surrounding community. According to Gerstein, the team "consciously decided it's not a business school. It's a school that uses entrepreneurship to engage kids into becoming citizens of their community—they create goods and services to serve the community and really study the community in order to make it better." The design team for the school put considerable thought into how their school would help the youth in their local context. Gerstein continues, "We had a lot of kids who were very, very passive. Ours was a neighborhood school; it had been a last resort. And entrepreneurs can't afford to be passive. So even if we have kids who never actually start a business, at least they're close to it, have core skills, and we have taken them from one point to another and they are able to be better citizens of their community."

The design team also saw the practical benefits of the particular lens they were developing for their school. In many low-income communities, "you may have to work for somebody else, and they could have a business on the side. In a lot of low-income communities, people have side businesses in order to make ends meet." To fulfill their vision, they connect students with community entrepreneurs, banks, and a small business development center. This makes the learning relevant and meets a larger community-oriented goal. Having the ability to create and sustain small businesses also supports students as they contemplate paying for postsecondary education. Schools that understand the needs of their students are more successful in implementing changes and remain more focused during implementation.

The West Clermont School District, the fifth-largest school district in the greater Cincinnati area, provides another example of the value of a clear, contextually relevant focus. West Clermont was a two–high school district, with both schools enrolling slightly more than thirteen hundred students, 97 percent of whom are white and 16 percent of whom are eligible for free or reduced-price lunch. In the fall of 2004, West Clermont opened ten new small autonomous schools, five in each building. In the materials used to educate the community and inform students who had to make a choice of new schools, the West Clermont school district provided distinct visions of the new schools and directly addressed the questions of what students would experience in each school, what skills they would develop, how their interests would be engaged, and what graduation requirements they would face. The information provided about the School of Technology and Communications exemplifies the approach. Exhibit 5.1 lists the questions posed to students considering that school.

The district also gave residents a sense of the big picture, communicating the overarching view of how each of the options benefits students in today's economy and diverse society. For example:

The School of Communications and Technology will focus on student interests in the field of communications and technology as it relates to broadcasting, journalism, writing, public speaking, visual arts and design, and computer technology, including programming.

Hands-on activities, seminars, and collaborative efforts will be the staples for student learning. Independent study will also be available. One-on-one mentor relationships spanning the entire high school experience will ensure that the individual learning styles of students are met.

All student learning and experiences will be authentic; that is, students will work on projects with real life application. They will see products through from start to finish, building multi-genre portfolios. They

---

EXHIBIT 5.1

Choosing a School: One Option

Is the School of Communications and Technology right for you?

1. Do you think it would be cool to learn how to design Web pages?

2. Do you wish you were a really good photographer?

3. Do you want to know how a newspaper is produced?

4. Can you see yourself as a TV producer some day?

5. Would you like to be able to support yourself as a freelance writer someday?

6. Do you listen to a lot of music and go to a lot of movies?

7. Did you love *The Matrix?*

8. Do you like to get into discussions with your friends about what constitutes good music?

9. Do you like messing around with video games, trying to figure out different ways to win?

10. Do you get more of a kick watching commercials than watching the TV shows?

Source: *West Clermont Local School District, 2001, p. 20.*

will identify communications-related problems and then work to develop and implement solutions.

The district offered specific descriptions framed with their rationale for the sweeping change, referred to the need for schools to educate for the current economy, to address poor graduation rates and mediocre test scores, and to create a positive school climate that academically challenges students.

Strengths and Challenges of Career-Based Approaches

Schools that could be considered career schools are among the most common types of new school being created, but they are also controversial. Anecdotal evidence suggests that career-oriented schools are the ones most likely to have difficulties in implementing a vision and curricular approach because it is easy for a school to launch into connections with specific career partners (for example, a School of Health working with a local hospital) without thinking through the school's overall curriculum and pedagogy.

Educators we interviewed raised additional concerns about a career-based approach. First, some careers are seen as more or less prestigious and tend to be more or less lucrative. Many careers are also strongly segmented by sex, race, and class. Based on these broad social patterns, schools may be chosen preferentially by one group of students or another, resulting in a *de facto*, if unintentional, system of tracking. Unless there's an active attempt to address stereotypes about who can and should attend which schools, it's fairly predictable that schools of technology or of physical science, for example, will draw a disproportionate number of boys; the arts will be a strong draw for girls; global studies may draw students from other countries.

Second, some educators are concerned that career-themed schools may create a perception that students' future careers are dictated by their high school's focus. Students who do not get into the medical career school, for example, may believe that their chance of becoming a doctor has been diminished or that if they do attend they will be less likely to have access to a career outside medicine. Such concerns may create considerable resistance to the general notion of small, focused schools, in favor of the comprehensive high school, which may be perceived as keeping all options open for all students.

On the other hand, the career-theme approach has undeniable assets. Career focuses may attract parents and students by providing a clear link between what is learned at school and familiar work trajectories and social contexts. Michael Klonsky, director of the Small Schools Workshop in Illinois (which is helping local Chicago high schools through the conversion process), underscores this need: "The problem with many schools today is that students do not see the link between their school work and the future. Kids want to do something important now. So while career academies are one way, and an obvious way, to create this link to the future, the important idea is to have a curricular focus that leads somewhere." Career or work connections can tap into student interest in a different way to make students engaged and provide clear reasons to stay in school as they create pathways to the future. The work of organizations such as Big Picture Company and Jobs for the Future that use apprenticeship are based on research and experience that indicates the need for and power of real-world learning. Both provide students with specific skills and knowledge and engage those students who have not fared well in conventional classrooms through active work-based learning.

Curriculum that provides training in relevant careers can serve another very practical purpose: it provides students with skills to earn a livelihood that will enable them to continue studying, if they so choose. East Cleveland's Shaw High has a number of successful vocational programs—a cosmetology program, for example, and a fire science program that prepares students to take the state test to become fire fighters. Sharon Brown, a coach at the school, notes:

> *This community, being very poor, really wants their children to be successful in education—and successful defined as being employable as well as being able to go on to college. . . . There are a number of young women in the cosmetology program—very bright young women, good students—who opted for cosmetology because they know they can make enough money to pay their way through college. They can articulate their strategy very, very clearly: "I study cosmetology because I can pay my way through college doing this. I've seen other people do it."*

Career-themed schools have also been seen as advantageous because they tend to galvanize stakeholder support. A number of initiatives found that career themes made the idea of conversion more tangible; the potential mission of a school named "Physical Science" is easier to communicate than that of one named "Beacon."

Instructional Vision and Special Needs

Developing a school's instructional vision and practice is an important step in the process of creating a vision. This is especially true when thinking about the needs of students who require additional support. Conversion schools often find it difficult to provide appropriate services to students currently identified as needing special services, such as special education students or English language learners.

Of course, large comprehensive high schools also have this problem. The key for practitioners in working with these groups of students is to accurately identify which students need unique supports, identify what services they need, and then develop a whole school design and instructional approach that will support unique populations while also strengthening the learning outcomes of all students.

Special Education Students

The term *special education* is used to refer to students who encompass a wide range of circumstances—from mild, moderate, to severe learning, emotional, or physical disabilities. A first challenge for conversion schools is to develop an approach to properly and equitably assess students. Advocacy groups, such as the Civil Rights Project at Harvard University (2002), have presented a body of evidence that indicate certain racial groups—particularly African American and Native Americans—are persistently overrepresented and misclassified in the special education arena, and often receive inferior services. Individual bias and bias in evaluation tools contributes to the mislabeling of youth of color and has to be actively monitored and countered. For example, educators have reported cases where temporary or correctable social, emotional, and behavioral problems are diagnosed as severe learning or mental disabilities.

Once the type and level of needs among special education students is accurately identified, conversion and small school leaders can develop designs and instructional approaches to support all students. Students who failed in a conventional classroom, who were pulled out for behavioral issues that were social and emotional in nature, have responded to engaging active pedagogy of small schools. They blossom with the intense personalization of low student:teacher ratios and daily advisories with a curriculum to support social and emotional needs. Small schools are also able to differentiate instruction and teach to multiple learning styles in a way that allows for inclusion of students with a wider range of learning disabilities.

Some small schools, like the Boston Arts Academy (BAA), have created an approach that supports full inclusion for special education students, providing them full access to the regular education curriculum. BAA strives for a seamless blending of curriculum and teaching strategies. To that end, staff are trained in adaptive pedagogies such as differentiated instruction that support heterogeneous classrooms and help teachers adjust their teaching modes to meet students where they are. Special education teachers at BAA

- Take part in content area meetings.

- Work with content area teachers to plan curriculum and instruction.

- Co-teach curriculum with content area teachers.

In addition, BAA has partnered with a local college to create a dual certification program, so regular education teachers are adding certificates in special education. This allows further flexibility in the ways that they can co-teach with each other.

For this work to be seamless it is critical that teachers have substantial daily common planning and problem-solving time. Teachers do need time to plan together, to discuss the unique needs of each student, and to modify or adapt curricula to support each student's learning goals and learning style.

Another example, discussed in Chapter Three, occurred at Fenway High School in Boston. Fenway recognized the need to help students with emotional and social needs such as anorexia, depression, or suicidal gestures. Its staff also realized that all their students could benefit from having individuals at the school trained in counseling. Fenway consequently redesigned its student support staff, hiring people with clinical experience and moving from the traditional guidance counselor role—addressing the postsecondary aspirations of students—to a role of running advisories and supporting teachers in doing so, as well as making connections for students and parents with local clinics and neighborhood services. The school trained other staff to take on the more traditional roles of the guidance counselors.

English Language Learners

As schools contemplate and plan their conversions, and as new small schools develop their visions, it is vital that schools fully understand the needs of ELL students. Here are just some of the issues schools must grapple with:

- Accurately identifying *which* students have English language learning needs

- Accurately identifying the *type* and *level* of needs (that is, understanding the difference between English language acquisition and English language development and literacy, and the strategies that are necessary and effective with each)

- Finding staff with appropriate training or finding resources to train existing staff

- Understanding and addressing the social, cultural, and political context that affects English language acquisition, literacy, and development

As schools more clearly understand the needs of their students, they also need models of school visions that serve English language learners effectively.

Laurie Olsen, executive director of California Tomorrow, has seen four conversion models that support the needs of students who require language acquisition support:

- A newcomer academy, in which students are supported until they gain the skills needed to attend a mainstream school

- A model where teachers with bilingual certification work across each of the new schools

- A model where one or more schools are specifically established for and devoted to students who need language acquisition support, in the manner of International High School in New York City

- A model where one or more small schools devote attention to dual language acquisition, such as the Marble Hill School for International Studies in New York City

The benefits of the fourth approach are that it makes language an asset and builds off the strengths of students. It supports the acquisition of another language for both English speakers and English language learners, and it provides a clear vision, instructional mission, and professional development support plans for a school. This approach also establishes a distinct school climate of inclusion that explicitly creates equity between cultures and languages. We address issues of how student choice and equity are affected by the overall array of school designs generated in a district in Chapter Eleven.

An Open Approach to School Formation

Thus far, we've discussed issues of creating a school vision in a process where the design team identifies a vision or curricular focus before opening the new small school. As an alternative to creating a vision and then creating new schools, however, communities can open new schools and then create the school's vision.

Clover Park High School, in Lakewood, Washington, near Seattle, for example, is using a "get small" approach. Clover Park serves about sixteen hundred students (47 percent white, 24 percent black, 17 percent Asian, and 11 percent Hispanic, with 39 percent eligible for free or reduced-price lunch) and is now in its third year of the conversion process. The faculty randomly divided the school into four groups of teachers and students, each of which was to become a new school. Each randomly formed group was then responsible for creating its school's vision and developing its instructional focus.

Clover Park's school coach, Holli Hanson, sees this approach as "more organic." She says, "The group sits down and says, 'OK, we're here. Now what is our vision and our mission?' The group has to talk these things through, because they don't have a predetermined theme to hang their hat on."

Using this approach, teams typically take longer to develop a school's identity than they do in the other approaches described. As Hanson suggests, this extra time may well allow for the conversations to go deeper. Further, it allows the staff time to try out different curricular approaches or strategies before settling on something. Clover Park is now in its third year of grade-level exhibitions. For these exhibitions, staff are experimenting with different foci, such as social justice and careers, to discover what they feel passionate about and what seems most powerful for student learning.

Final Questions to Consider

We believe that both approaches—deciding on a particular vision and curricular focus before a school opens or waiting for them to emerge organically from the predilections of a given faculty and students—are potentially effective; both approaches clearly have trade-offs. What appears to be key is that the school identity, vision, or curricular focus serves to concentrate and deepen a school's attention on teaching and learning for its whole student population. Vision drives the development of distinct, innovative, effective school design.

Based on lessons learned from the process for conversions to date, here are three questions to keep in mind when considering a school vision and curricular identity:

- With the specific needs of your students in mind, what are your main priorities? To connect students to school; to connect students to the community; to connect students to work; or connect students with college? If your goal is to connect students to work that can be attained without a college degree, how will the school avoid the pitfall of effectively "tracking" its students off of a path toward college?

- How do you ensure that the vision, curricular identity, and culture help promote high expectations for all students?

- How do you ensure that the array of school visions and designs are equitable in how they, as a comprehensive system of schools, meet the needs of all students in the district or the preconversion large school? For example, does the overall array of options available to students remedy or reinforce patterns of racial, economic, or cultural inequity and segregation?

Chapter 6
Transforming Instructional Practice

ONE OF THE MOST difficult challenges of large high school conversions is developing and enhancing teachers' pedagogical practices to improve engagement, learning, and achievement. Many of the first high schools to begin conversion efforts spent considerably more time on issues of school design than on those of professional development, such as ongoing in-school collaboration with other teachers, visits to other small schools, and formal training designed to strengthen instruction. Consequently, after restructuring, teachers had the conditions that allowed them to personalize and transform their teaching, but they struggled to implement the necessary classroom pedagogy. Drawing on the experience of schools and the wisdom of coaches and researchers, this chapter explores ways to build the foundation for improved academic outcomes and student growth as schools make the shift from large to small. Here are two key ideas for improving instruction as schools transform:

- Identify the pedagogical practices that will enable your school to meet the needs of its students.

- Develop the capacity of teachers to engage in these practices. This will involve developing a shared vision of effective teaching and learning in small schools, and then providing professional development to build targeted skills.

Small School Pedagogy

The challenge of opening small autonomous schools makes it easy to forget that the opening of the school is not an endpoint but a beginning. The opening of a new small autonomous school provides a renewed opportunity to teach all students well. As researcher Michelle Fine states, small schools shouldn't be "big schools in drag"—schools with the culture and learning environment of large schools. The opportunities created by a small school cannot be realized if the style of teaching remains the same as it was in the old large one. Conversion goals will not be realized if, for example, teachers continue to teach lecture style, even when they have a class small enough to be a seminar, or the relationships between and among students and teachers remain the same, even though teachers could personalize their practice, or principals continue to run schools like big bureaucracies with a hierarchical chain of command, even though they have the opportunity to distribute leadership.

While the exact nature of a community's new small schools will be unclear at the beginning of the conversion process, we do know that certain elements characterize effective small schools: heterogeneous classes and differentiated instruction, block schedules, advisories, personalized practice, an authentic curriculum, adaptive pedagogy, performance assessment, and anti-racist teaching. (Many of these practices are discussed in Chapter Two and listed in the School Redesign Network list of ten features of effective small schools in Appendix D.) We also are learning, thanks in part to the evaluation research on the implementation of the Gates Foundation high school redesign grants (American Institutes for Research & SRI International, 2003, 2004), that predictable challenges confront many small start-up schools. In particular, small start-up schools need a sustained focus on instruction and curriculum development and on preserving equity while working with students of varying prior academic achievement. Small schools developing out of a large high school conversion not only face these same challenges around instruction and equity, they also confront a standing school culture and vision of pedagogy that usually conflicts with or undermines the conditions sought in the new school.

Tom Vander Ark, executive director of education at the Bill & Melinda Gates Foundation, believes that struggling schools not only need a different structure but a markedly different mission and culture. However, in a school that is converting from large to small in the original building and with the same staff and students, changing these elements is extremely difficult. According to Vander Ark, changing a school culture that is complacent with inequitable outcomes requires a disruption in the school's practices and expectations. Frequently, existing beliefs about different types of students need to be consciously interrupted as well. Many conversion efforts have focused on structural changes to create this disruption. Ultimately, however, the change must affect classroom practice. When teacher collaboration and professional training time focus on improving instruction, besides changing school culture, the effort provides an opportunity for this disruption and is an essential lever for change.

Developing Vision Develops Capacity

If we know what small schools look like, how do we get there? Instructional practice should drive design. As Kate Jamentz, former executive director of the School Redesign Network, says, "We need to put teaching at the center of the structure conversation." A solid pedagogical foundation and vision for the school makes design more effective. Instructional practice is based on the needs of students, and discussions and decisions about design should happen in the context of professional development on instructional practice and student needs. Pedagogical support—training to help teachers take advantage of personalized schools and classrooms—can and should be embedded throughout the conversion process.

Eric Nadelstern of the New York City Department of Education says:

You need to know what you believe about how kids learn, and everything about how you conduct business in that school needs to reflect those beliefs. That's the degree of coherence that will allow the teachers to ensure that the kids are successful. But the primary thing, really, is to get a group of people who believe something together about how kids learn and then give them an opportunity not only to realize that but to ensure that they prove the efficacy of that approach by ensuring that the kids succeed. Because in the end, it's the connection between the teachers and the kids.

Helping teachers develop their vision of how students learn and what relationships enable that learning is an important part of professional development that supports powerful instruction.

While we know the characteristics of many effective small schools, each school community must still spend time developing its own beliefs of instructional practice. This supports school staff in shaping the school vision of how to engage students and helps teachers own the need for a certain pedagogy. The small school provides the opportunity—perhaps only glimpsed by the school community at the beginning of the process—to transform instruction to best meet the needs of all students. Because it's only glimpsed, teachers need time to engage and develop their vision. Building the vision for small schools is an important step and an opportunity for professional development in the kind of teaching that can occur in small schools.

Professional development time is most effective when it focuses heavily on instructional practice, integrates that focus in conversations on the conversion process and, in fact, allows it to drive structure, culture, and design decisions. The experience of Clover Park High School supports this idea. School coach Holli Hanson saw that teachers were getting burned out by the effort of making decisions about structural issues, and they were not making decisions that related to their classrooms or instruction techniques. The school was making design decisions without having spent the time to develop a unified school vision and a vision of instructional practice. Hanson led the school staff through a *futures protocol,* a structured conversation that is often used in the early stages of creating a plan or project to expand and clarify the vision of what a group or individual is really trying to accomplish. Seven or eight major themes emerged around what the staff wanted their school to evolve into in the future.

According to Hanson:

Based on the results of the futures protocol, we saw some nuts-and-bolts things that we turned into action groups and people got to decide which of those action groups they were in. We also pulled out two major instructional focuses that they focused on all year. So some of every early release day is devoted to staff development around reading and inquiry. That has seemed to be the one thing about which people can say, "OK, I'm excited to be here because I'm going to learn something new. I'm going to have something to take away to my classroom."

In Lakewood, Washington, Clover Park's teachers were still working in a large school as they developed visions for their new small schools. The staff were engaged in professional development designed to support practices that they would most often use in their small schools. At the same time, they walked out of the current professional development session with something they could use right away. They were becoming more comfortable with the pedagogy they would be implementing, while at the same time building support for the small schools as they saw how the current school structure inhibited the power of their new practice.

The school has also done several "learning walks" and staff observations to see what people are doing in their classrooms around reading. By making their practice public, they increased their collaboration as well as generated ideas and scaffolding. Hanson concludes, "If we really want that powerful instruction, it takes awhile to build that."

This sort of discussion on instructional practice and vision can drive school design when redesign opportunities arise. For example, the Marble Hill School for International Studies, the first of four small autonomous schools at John F. Kennedy High School, is the only school in New York City with a population split 50–50 between English language learners and English-fluent students. The school opened in September 2002 with a hundred ninth graders, 64 percent of whom were Hispanic. The ELL students learn English and the English speakers must learn a second language. School staff believed that it was important to require all students to learn a second language. This core component of the school establishes a culture of equity and respect between different racial and ethnic groups.

Iris Zucker, the principal, explains the school's vision and how the design supports that vision: "It's an international studies school with a rigorous academic program, a focus of college and beyond. We want them to learn a second language; we want them to do international studies." Zucker praised the school's block schedule, which allows ELL teachers to collaborate with subject-area teachers, a partnership that shakes up their traditional alliances, allows teachers to share their knowledge and discuss the needs of each student, supports all students as they learn, and supports the mission and vision of the school.

Professional Development in Targeted Skills

The pedagogical change necessary to capitalize on the opportunities that small schools afford is challenging even to flexible and adaptable educators. Change on this scale raises uncertainty. Teachers want to know: "What's expected of me? Can I do this? How will I be supported?" Lack of familiarity with the teaching now expected of them—and the lack of a concrete plan to address their needs—is a major challenge to staff developing a sense of ownership over the creation of small autonomous schools.

But given our knowledge of what successful small schools look like, it is straightforward to identify where anxiety is focused or gaps in proficiency exist—such as around teaching heterogeneous classes or implementing performance assessments—and plan backwards to develop skills and generate ownership among teachers in the emerging small school. Training or discussions around the skills they need to teach and collaborate in a small school increases the comfort of teachers (and other community members) and ensures they are able to take advantage of the unfolding opportunities that small schools present for powerful instruction and learning. This is not to say that everyone will immediately become adept at new teaching strategies— the process is long and hard—but the support, and a plan for sustaining that support, increases both commitment and the likelihood of success.

Bill Hart, principal of the 1250-student Leominster High School in central Massachusetts, which enrolls a student population that is 77 percent white and 15 percent Hispanic and has 18 percent of its students eligible for free or reduced-price lunch, was asked by his staff to present an example of just what a complex of six autonomous schools might look like as the school community contemplated conversion. He presented to the staff a plan that showed teacher assignments, numbers of students in each school, and schedules. This plan was useful for staff to visualize what their experience would be like, and as a result, many teachers were able to articulate their worries early in the conversion process. In the case of Leominster, some faculty voiced grave concerns about moving to a block schedule; many had previously had negative experiences with this design feature. Principal Hart, supported by Meg Anderson, an external coach from the Center for Collaborative Education in Boston, and Frank Honts, director of the Regional Teachers Center at the Francis W. Parker Essential Charter School, was able to design professional development that directly addressed this concern.

In another case, a teacher needed clarity around and capacity built on the specific issue of performance assessment. Jan Reeder, director of the CES Northwest Center, recounts the story of a thirty-year veteran teacher who was not yet convinced that small schools were needed. After a workshop on performance assessments, a key feature in the design of their new school, this teacher admitted that he had not known how to integrate such assessments into his teaching, which contributed to his concern about small schools. Once he felt more comfortable with the new techniques and believed he had the support to master them, he favored the conversion.

Heterogeneous Classrooms

The small school movement is about creating more personalized communities where adults and students know each other well. In effective small schools, students are successfully educated in heterogeneous classrooms. A challenge in conversion schools has been in building the capacity of school staff to use differentiated instruction to teach in a heterogeneous classroom, supporting students of varying ability levels and needs.

Creating the small student:teacher loads and school communities, while important, just establishes the conditions where teachers can meet students' needs effectively. Teachers still require considerable support in understanding how to take advantage of the powerful opportunities offered by increased personalization (for example, it helps them identify and respond to specific student needs and provide social and emotional supports) and for teacher collaboration (to share knowledge and co-develop strategies for individual students, as well as to enable the development of literacy strategies across content areas). This is especially necessary to support special education students and English language learners, who, while they also benefit from the personalized community, need to work with teachers trained in supporting their specific needs.

Many educators we spoke with discussed the need of helping teachers to develop a larger repertoire of adaptive pedagogical strategies to meet the challenge of working in heterogeneous classrooms. The School Redesign Network at Stanford University defines *adaptive pedagogy* as the way successful teachers adjust their teaching modes to meet students where they are. This requires moving from the traditional high school lecture approach to allow for multiple learning styles, opportunities for group work, explicit teaching of academic skills, and personalized additional support. For example, schools have developed their capacity in supporting and developing multiple intelligences and in establishing differentiated instruction.

Another area for developing capacity is the "universal design for learning" (UDL), developed by the Center for Applied Special Technology, a system of teaching, learning, and assessment that allows students with different learning styles and needs to work productively in a single classroom. UDL represents educational methods and materials that are flexible and powerful enough to help all students, regardless of ability, maximize their progress. The central practical premise of UDL is that a curriculum should include alternatives to make it accessible and appropriate for individuals with different backgrounds, learning styles, abilities, and disabilities in widely varied learning contexts. The *universal* in universal design does not imply one optimal solution for everyone. Rather, it reflects an awareness of the unique nature of each learner and the need to accommodate differences, creating learning experiences that suit the learners as individuals and maximize each learner's ability to progress. In a UDL Learning classroom, students and teachers use

- Multiple modes of representing the material
- Multiple ways of engaging with the materials
- Multiple modes of expressing learning

To help teachers develop and enhance appropriate skills, it is necessary to understand the specific needs, particularly in terms of the language acquisition and development, learning disabilities, or social or emotional challenges of all of their students. In Chapter Five we discussed unique issues related to special education and English language learners, and strategies that small schools can use to support social and emotional needs through personalization and advisories, often in ways that are a driving part of their whole school design. These strategies allow the schools to address the needs of these unique populations while also strengthening the learning environment for all students.

For example, the many students classified as ELL are far from alone in needing language development and literacy support. English literacy issues arise for students for whom English is a first language. The issue of identifying how many students need support or should be considered ELL is complicated because many high school students not classified as ELL are fluent orally but not in academic English, and many students whose first language is English are far behind grade level in its use. Indeed, many large schools are choosing to convert precisely because they want to address the needs of students who are a number of grade levels behind in reading and writing. Such students need considerable language development and literacy support.

Finding the Time for Conversations That Lead to Real Change

Most schools have used their existing contract-specified professional development time for these discussions, but some schools and districts have created more time. One coach described working in a district attempting high school conversion that had six contracted days but had not supported finding more. Not surprisingly, this district struggles mightily through the conversion effort. Another district had committed to ongoing professional development time during the school's weekly early release. They spent three days focusing on instructional practice and one with design as the main focus. This time has helped the school have the kinds of conversation its people feel they need to move forward.

Support organizations and external coaches have generally observed that districts that create more time for teachers and the community to engage in these conversations are more likely to move the work forward. Some efforts have been able to do so through adding more release days, focusing discussions during collaborative time during the day, or providing critical friends group (CFG) training for teachers. CFG training promotes adult growth by helping teachers take better advantage of the collaborative time and structures available by focusing conversations directly on student learning.

Challenges to Integrating Pedagogical Support and Design Planning

At least three significant challenges make it difficult to provide pedagogical support during conversion efforts. First, teachers are often reluctant to talk about pedagogy, the personal relationships and beliefs at the core of teaching, especially if they don't know each other well. This is true whether a school is involved in a conversion effort or not. Second, during conversions, especially in the early stages, design seems to be a more pressing issue. Third, participants tend to have the overwhelming feeling (and often face the reality) that time is short.

Schools and districts in the conversion process continue to move forward, balancing multiple demands. Our research indicates that it is possible to find more time or other resources, and it is possible, as detailed in some of the examples given in this chapter, to more fully integrate instructional practice, professional development, school vision, and school structure. The tension some feel between attending to design issues or to instructional practice can create a false dichotomy. Rather, effective and appropriate instruction is the lens through which one can view all conversion decisions. In that way, each step in the process is an opportunity for professional development—and an opportunity for change. What's important to remember is that a good school is always one that is on a journey of reflection and improvement. Questions of instructional practice and student needs are always at the forefront of discussions in good schools, and the conversion process can help schools develop and strengthen these characteristics.

Chapter 7

Essentials of Small School Leadership

RICHARD ELMORE (2002) articulates a perspective on leadership that's relevant to small schools: educational leadership today has only one real goal—to ensure that instruction enables all students in the school to succeed. According to effective small school leaders, what *leadership* means in a small school is qualitatively different from what it means in a large comprehensive school. Large comprehensive schools, because of their size, structure, and culture, have largely focused on school management; small schools provide the opportunity for leaders to focus on the school's educational mission. A notion of leadership that focuses on the educational mission suggests both a different set of leadership tasks—and a much broader definition of who is included in school leadership.

A key task of conversion is to prepare members of the existing school community for their part in leading the small school. The research on school design and on current effective leaders themselves paints a clear picture of leadership in successful small schools—and of how it differs from the vision of leadership typically found in large schools. Conversion teams face characteristic considerations, strategies, and challenges as they design their new leadership structures and select and support educators and parents to fill those roles.

Leadership Differences in Small and Large Schools

Just as small schools afford the possibility of a different kind of teaching and learning, they also afford the possibility of a different kind of leadership. The structure and size of a large school makes personalized leadership strategies impossible. Our research suggests that for small schools to be successful in achieving college readiness for all students, leadership strategies need to differ significantly from what is typical in a large school. We note two main differences between small and large school leadership: instructional leadership versus management, and distributive leadership versus hierarchical leadership.

Instructional Leadership Versus Management

All schools require management: they have budgets to track, buses to schedule, vendors to pay, personnel to hire, a building to maintain, and much more. However, in recent years, the literature on leadership for school reform has been dominated by the notion of the principal as "instructional leader"—the idea that rather than seeing their primary function as the handling of managerial tasks, principals would focus on teaching and learning, and their key role would be to coach teachers in their work.

Unfortunately, in a school with a large student population and extensive facilities, faculty, and course offerings, the management or administrative tasks are so numerous—and support often so limited—that principals frequently find that this aspect of their job consumes all their time and attention. Small schools still have plenty to manage, but the idea of a principal serving as instructional leader is more viable there because of the smaller numbers of students and staff. Deborah Meier, founder of Central Park East Secondary School in New York and co-founder of the Coalition of Essential Schools, has argued that a school faculty should be no larger than the number of people who can comfortably sit around a large table. This size allows the faculty to know each other well, creating enormous potential for providing support where it is needed and for combining complementary strengths. It provides an opportunity to collaborate, discuss student assessments, and develop individual and schoolwide instructional improvement strategies. The potential for this kind of synergy is one of a small school's great strengths, and helping to nurture it is a key role of the principal.

According to Larry Myatt in Boston, small school leaders must have technical and leadership skills that are both deep and broad. Principals of large comprehensive high schools often oversee scores of teachers, administrators, and school support staff. Often assistant principals are responsible for major components of school management, such as discipline or counseling. Because large school principals have assistant principals who can handle subsets of the job, these principals can develop specialties in some areas. Small school leaders often have only one other administrator and support staff person; they must have or develop deep knowledge of many areas of schooling. Myatt believes that small school leaders need to know about portfolio assessment, language acquisition, adaptive pedagogies, budget, operations, and ordering things; they need to know everyone, from custodians to parents. They need to understand how to use small school autonomies. They have to say hello to students in seven different languages, because they have that many languages spoken in their school. Their skill set cannot be wide and shallow: "You have to work over time very intimately with a lot of people. It's both a technical and a leadership skill set that a big school principal can duck." Exhibit 7.1 describes the qualities and skills of small school leaders.

Distributive Versus Hierarchical Leadership

A key distinction in the governance structure of a small school compared to a large comprehensive school is that it must cultivate and distribute leadership broadly throughout the school community, as opposed to making leadership something that rests in the hands of an individual or two, such as the principal and assistant principal. Indeed an essential role of a small school principal is to facilitate and support leadership among others. In small schools, leadership roles exist for many stakeholders—not just principals, but teacher-leaders, students, families, and community members as well.

The "distributed instructional leadership" model, in a snapshot, plays out in small schools through highly collaborative work among teachers who use data in cycles of inquiry that drive continual improvement of

---

EXHIBIT 7.1

Small School Leadership Requirements

- Developing and articulating a powerful vision for equity and achievement

- Creating and sustaining a professional learning community committed to inquiry and equity

- Focusing on instruction

- Supporting distributive leadership

- Using both program design and resource allocation to enhance equity and student learning

- Developing authentic partnerships with ethnically and linguistically diverse communities

- Understanding the change process and continuous school improvement cycle

Source: *Adapted from the Leading for Equity, Achievement and Democracy (LEAD) program, developed by BayCES.*

instruction for student mastery. Such schools have formal means for shared decision making, where examination of other staff members' practices and teaching—including observation of teaching and student work—is a core practice and part of ongoing professional development. Small school leaders need to know the instructional strategies that smallness allows and requires. They are not managers who can drop in once a year for a teacher evaluation; they are regular coaches, collaborative culture facilitators, and providers of professional development.

With distributive leadership, for example, teachers make their own decisions about when they take and how they spend the time and resources allotted to them for professional development. This approach assumes that given the right environment and incentives, teachers will use their direct knowledge of their own and their students' specific strengths and weaknesses to design a personalized professional development plan. For external opportunities, teachers work with their team or house to ensure that their classes are covered; internally, teachers use their shared common plan time to meet their needs and the needs of their team. They can, for example, develop curriculum or discuss how to meet the needs of individual students.

Small schools require that teachers take on leadership roles. Bill Gerstein, principal of South Shore High School's Entrepreneurship High School on Chicago's south side, says that in small schools, "You're shifting power from the principal to the teacher. What you're really looking for in the small school model are teachers who really want greater control, who want to step up and be leaders. That's not every teacher but it's more than you would ever imagine." For small schools to work, teachers need to take ownership and be committed to changes in the areas where they have most impact—in the nature of the relationship between teacher and student. They need to have a say about the conditions in the school that affect their ability to provide powerful instructional experiences.

It bears repeating: A governing principle of small schools is that the people most heavily affected by decisions are actively involved in making them. George Wood, principal of Federal Hocking High School, a 470-student school in Athens, Ohio, says, "Keep people close to their expertise and where they spend their time, and give lots of autonomy in these areas." If someone is in charge of maintenance in the school, we would expect that person would have significant input into decisions around repair priorities and hiring maintenance personnel. Similarly, students and teachers, most central to the learning process, would have significant decision-making power regarding particular subjects to be taught and how they are taught. However, it might be an unwise use of scarce time and resources to get an entire leadership team involved in ordering paper for the copier or other supplies like that. How an individual school's governance structure sets priorities for using collaborative time will vary, but experienced small school leaders believe priorities should be set based on what it takes to reach the ultimate educational mission of the school.

Developing Leadership Capacity of Teachers, Students, Parents, and Community Members

In small schools, every stakeholder—parent, student, teacher, community member—plays a role in supporting and sustaining the school.

The work of developing leadership capacity brings clarity to the changing role of the principal as instructional leaders. . . . Today's effective principal constructs a shared vision with members of the school community, convenes the conversations, insists on student learning focus, evokes and supports leadership in others, models and participates in collaborative practices; helps pose the questions and facilitates dialogue that addresses the confounding issues of practice. This work requires skill and new understanding; it is much easier to tell or to manage than it is to perform as a collaborative instructional leader [Lambert, 2002, p. 40].

Michelle Kennedy, teacher-leader of the Math, Science, and Technology Academy (MAST), a high school of about three hundred students located in the Glen Este High School campus in Cincinnati, Ohio, says: "Leaders create an atmosphere where if they're not there somebody else will take on that role and the school's mission and vision will carry on. I have a counselor who has been a right-hand person to me. There is another person who is ready to step into my role as small school coordinator. And I have about five to seven other people that take or will take a lead role." Many schools are launched by charismatic leaders, but for school and student success over time, leaders have to be replaceable.

Beyond the teacher-leader roles and collaboration already mentioned, distributed leadership plays out practically in curriculum committees that include students, parents, and community members. These stakeholders can provide resources or serve as participants and judges in students' public demonstrations of mastery. Students can also write the student handbook, have a say in hiring staff, and be involved in student-led fairness committees that make a wide range of decisions and policies around discipline and codes of behavior. Please refer back to Chapter Four for a more thorough discussion of community leadership.

Potential Problems with Distributed Leadership

Some teachers hesitate to take on the roles defined in a distributed instructional leadership model. According to Wagner (2001), teachers may resist such change from the general human tendency to avoid risks and hesitancy about change, or from being accustomed to a culture and structure of professional expertise, or from burnout, or from placing a positive value on autonomy and isolation. Whatever the reasons, not all teachers will be drawn to practices such as engaging in collaborative cycles of inquiry and peer observation of classrooms. If such collegial practices are to become part of the new school culture, one of the roles of the leaders is to address obstacles and concerns about distributed leadership. Directors need to find ways to make these practices truly valuable to the faculty—through developing a shared vision and by supporting acquisition of the skills necessary to adopt these practices.

According to Michelle Kennedy, "Leadership is essential for the collaborative culture you need for a successful school. Leaders help create the environment where people are willing to work together, people feel open, people feel 'Yes, I can take this risk and it's OK.'" Leaders create a culture that encourages risk taking, one where teachers' professional development needs are met, and where collaboration replaces isolation and a professional learning community can develop. Of course, the school may have some teachers who really do not want to be part of a more collaborative environment. In such cases, the leader may work with them to choose schools that better match their work style preferences.

While teachers generally welcome the opportunity to be more involved in decisions about curriculum and instruction, they tend to reject participating in decisions that are not closely related to teaching. The principal faces a bit of a balancing act in inviting teachers to participate in decisions about the school and protecting them from what they might experience as administrivia. Indeed, creating a leadership structure that evokes the most creative input from all members of the school community requires leadership—and also a good deal of management.

Selecting and Developing Conversion Small School Leaders

When planning the leadership of the new small schools, the question inevitably arises: What role will the current principal of the comprehensive high school take on? Some large school principals make the transition and become excellent small school leaders; others are not interested or may not be strong candidates to do so. Some large school principals are involved in creating the new autonomous schools and plan on becoming a building principal, supporting all of the new small schools (we discuss the implications of this in more depth in Chapter Eleven). Other principals manage much of the conversion process, then move into the district office. As noted, the comprehensive high school principal at Tyee High School will assume a position of "conversion principal," handling many administrative details and problems that arise. This position is transitional only and will be eliminated after one year, replaced by a campus manager. The key is to devise a plan that takes advantage of the skills and gains the enthusiastic support of the principal while ensuring that new small schools acquire the autonomy and develop the leadership they need.

Strategies for Selecting Small School Leaders

Conversion efforts typically require a process for selecting, training, and supporting new small school leaders, to fit into the leadership structures devised by each new small school. Our research has indicated that questions about what type of formal leadership roles will be created and how individuals will be selected and supported in their development are unavoidably linked to practical questions about who is currently available for such roles. What capacity do the real-life candidates have, and what type of formal credentialing do they require?

A range of formal leadership structures and processes are available for conversion small schools, including a principal, co-directors, site committees, teacher collaboratives, and community involvement in hiring. In the co-director, committee, or collaborative models, labor is usually divided so that, for example, one director or teacher-leader takes primary responsibility for instructional leadership and the other takes greater responsibility for management and external relations. Formal or informal roles for teacher-leaders and instructional facilitators have been developed in a range of ways. Some efforts explicitly create new kinds of leadership positions that do not require administrative credentials, such as a formal position of lead teacher or in-house facilitator. Others are developing new credentialing processes for teachers, so those without administrative credentials can take formal leadership roles in new schools.

We have seen three ways that leaders have been found in the face of these constraints. In some situations, only current administrators at the converting school were considered for small school leadership roles. Other conversions set up a process in which anyone with a credential could apply. And in still others, distributive leadership roles were formally created for teachers who might not have an administrative credential.

Further, we have identified three key constraints for finding formal administrative leaders in the conversion movement. First, it can be difficult to identify individuals with the attitudes, skills, and knowledge necessary for effective small school leadership. Second, the new leaders must have any administrative credential needed for the district. Third, very few credentialing programs train someone specifically to be a leader of a small autonomous school, so many who try to gain the required credential receive training that is not geared to the challenge they face.

Current Administrators at the Converting School Only

One approach we saw for selecting leaders was a de facto decision by the central office that principals or assistant principals of the large schools would become the principals of the small schools. The assumption that the large school leaders would lead the new schools was unquestioned, and no formal application process occurred. While this choice appears straightforward and simple, we found that after the fact, people involved in school conversions often learned that not all principals or assistant principals had skills suited to running a small school. Conversion teams that focused on the differences in the leadership needs of small and large school were less likely to make the automatic choice of an assistant principal.

The lack of an open process had a number of consequences. On a general level it led to the selection of some school leaders who lacked attitudes or skills suited to leading a new small school. This undermined morale and inhibited the creation of a distinct culture of shared participatory decision making. In one facility housing a number of schools, for example, former assistant principals were given small school director positions but retained facility-wide duties that created a conflict between large facility and small school practices and loyalties. The problem with this approach is that it rarely (and then only by chance) chooses the best leader for a specific school.

Anyone with an Appropriate Credential

In this approach, anyone with an appropriate credential can apply for the position. Consequently, teachers who have administrative credentials are part of the pool of potential applicants. In some contexts, all department chairs have administrative credentials. In Leominster, Massachusetts, for example, the new principal of the first conversion school was a former department chair, selected through an open process. This is a more common, traditional model that is consistent with how most school leaders are selected. We note, however, that these credentials do not guarantee that the candidates possess small school leadership skills.

Formal Distributive Leadership Model

Although the legal necessity for principals to have an administrative credential creates some constraints, conversion teams are beginning to implement a third model. This approach is based on ideas of distributive leadership, in which leadership positions for teachers are created and built into the conversion process. For example, in the West Clermont district in Ohio, each small school has a credentialed director, but also a teacher-leader responsible for instructional leadership.

In Indianapolis, the plan is to have two co-directors. One, the academic dean, would come with credentials to evaluate teachers. The other is the facilitator of teaching and learning, and that person takes on the role of instructional coach at the small school. Indianapolis has deliberately worked to set up a process of creating leadership structure and leader selection and development practices based on local leader capacity and credentialing requirements. Right after deciding to create multiple small autonomous schools, stakeholders brainstormed challenges they faced and created work groups to address them. According to Daniel Baron, co-director of the National School Reform Faculty, a roles and responsibilities workgroup brought a proposal to the whole district leadership team, which reached consensus on the framework outlined at the beginning of this paragraph.

The proposal created the criteria and job descriptions and set up an open process—anyone with the stated qualifications can apply for those positions, and the small schools choose their leaders from the resulting pool. This is a formal distributive leadership structure, with the academic dean taking on the typical administrative leadership roles and the facilitator of teaching and learning taking on the instructional leadership role. In addition, the facilitator of teaching and learning is expected to work toward an emerging teacher leadership certification. At this point, the agreement is more general and open, because it is unclear what credential should be necessary. Even though the credential does not yet exist there, the three major local universities— Indiana University, IUPUI, and the University of Indianapolis—want to support the development of a credentialing program for small school leaders. Consequently, the job description includes criteria that applicants would be working toward whatever credentialing process emerges.

Impact of Leader Selection and Development

Who selects the leader for the new small school is important to the development of the school's identity and distinct new culture, and to the principal's understanding of the new working relationships and autonomies. In instances where the leadership has been appointed by central office staff without input from the small school staff—typically when the assistant principals are the de facto leaders—it has not been surprising that it has been harder to build and support a unique school culture. In other places, such as Indianapolis, it was easier: the conversion team created the criteria and job descriptions, people applied for those positions, and the new small school staff helped choose their leaders. Setting things up so school staff choose their own leaders has the effect of building culture and increasing the districts' and schools' understanding of autonomies, especially of governance.

Thomas Proctor High School (in Utica, New York) provides a good example of the importance of leadership selection. Utica enrolls about eighteen hundred students, of whom 67 percent are white, 20 percent black, 10 percent Hispanic, and 4 percent Asian, and 57 percent of whom are eligible for free or reduced-price lunch. According to Stephen Spring, their school coach, the leaders of Utica's four design teams function well and are making many important decisions. The teams have been given considerable decision-making responsibility and have embraced that spirit of shared decision making. Their decisions are made democratically—sometimes surprisingly so. During the interview process for selecting a leader of one of the new schools, for example, the team and the school board disagreed on the choice. Ultimately, the school board supported the idea that the teachers make the choices for their own school. This was an important step for the schools and district to internalize a new and very different relationship between the board and an individual small school faculty.

Creating Programs to Develop Leaders for Small Schools

One of the greatest challenges for conversion high schools is to develop leaders with the skills, experience, and credentials necessary to be effective small school leaders. Developing leadership is always a complex endeavor, and developing leaders in conversion efforts poses some unique challenges. Most of the potential new leaders currently work within the culture of a large comprehensive school.

A few programs have been designed to support the training and development of small school leaders. Three we identified include the Principal Residency Network (PRN), a collaboration of the Center for Collaborative Education, Northeastern University, and the Fenway Institute for Urban School Renewal; Leading for Equity, Achievement, and Democracy (LEAD), run by BayCES and university staff in California; and KnowledgeWorks, directed by George Wood and by Paul Schwarz, previous co-director of

Central Park East Secondary School in New York City. The Knowledge-Works program was established to support small school leaders specifically within the context of conversions.

The experienced small school leaders who designed each of these programs assert that small school leaders need to develop different skills and competencies from the set large school leaders require, and they believe that to the greatest possible extent, leaders should be trained through apprenticeship and mentoring with someone who is already an effective small school leader. In PRN, leaders-in-training have such an apprenticeship, working beside their mentor in a rigorous field experience.

KnowledgeWorks is supporting more than seventy new school leaders. Lacking enough small school leaders to act as one-on-one mentors, it has created an advisory system—with each adviser supporting up to ten new leaders. Serving those who already hold credentials, the advisers focus on leadership rather than on the management aspects of the job. Leaders of the KnowledgeWorks program suggest that hands-on experience at a small school is particularly important for leaders. With the best will in the world, people coming from large high schools inevitably have large school habits and attitudes that they need to recognize and generally replace. KnowledgeWorks believes that it is more difficult to alter habits than to establish and develop new visions.

Chapter 8

Handling Electives, AP Classes, and Other Access Issues

THE CURRICULAR GOALS of autonomous small schools are simple: helping young people learn to use their minds well, and preparing them for higher education, work, and citizenship. These goals apply to all students, although the means to these goals will vary as students themselves vary. As Theodore Sizer has written in the Common Principles of the Coalition of Essential Schools: "The aphorism 'less is more' dominates: curricular decisions should be guided by the aim of thorough student mastery and achievement rather than by an effort to merely cover content." Students should go into material in depth rather than try for broad coverage. School practice should be tailor-made to ensure that every group or class of students can master the material and skills. It turns out that the smallness and mission-driven aspect of autonomous small schools directly support them in pursuing this central intellectual purpose.

Schools remain "comprehensive" at the expense of their ability to provide a high-quality education for all students. Increasingly high dropout rates, low college entrance rates, and reported low levels of engaged learning and intellectual vibrancy among students all indicate that large comprehensive schools are unable to meet the needs of a majority of students. Although research indicates that small schools are better able to meet the needs of each student, and particularly low-income students and students of color, conversion efforts often encounter the following concerns from the school community:

- How does this change affect students' options to pursue activities and classes of interest to them? That is, are we going to lose elective classes?

- How does this change affect students' ability to pursue postsecondary education? That is, what about AP classes?

- Are we losing access to resources we need? That is, don't we miss resources we would have from a large school? Should we share classes, teachers, band, choir, and sports?

Designing Curriculum to Meet All Students' Needs

When small schools focus on creating their curriculum, they follow three principles: First, make the curriculum personalized rather than comprehensive. Then develop all school activities from its central intellectual mission. Finally, deliver a high-quality education to all students.

As discussed in Chapter Six, a school's curricular choices should be based on its vision and mission. The process and priorities involved in creating curriculum and courses in a small school differ from their counterparts in a large comprehensive school. Small schools should base decisions about course offerings on the curricular needs and focus that follow from their central educational vision. Some conversion schools have instead thought in terms of subtracting from the predecessor school's offerings, seeing the task as making tough choices to eliminate courses typically found in a comprehensive curriculum: cutting languages, maintaining fewer (or no) tracks, offering fewer arts classes. This can center the conversation on losing what exists rather than on how to achieve a vision of more effective education.

Electives: Personalization Not Comprehensiveness

The curriculum of the comprehensive high school is a great draw. Comprehensive high schools were designed to offer a little something to everyone. Many schools undergoing the conversion process still act like shrunken comprehensive high schools—trying to offer the full range of courses without the resources to do so. Not surprisingly, members of these school communities feel frustrated, missing out on the benefits of small schools while losing many of the benefits of large ones.

When converting to small schools, many people worry about access to elective classes, but the real issue is a choice between personalization and comprehensiveness. In describing conversations about this topic, one school change coach said:

> *People get it in increments, little by little. People bring a lot of big-school assumptions into their work and it just takes time for people to see things differently. [For example] this fall we were in a meeting with [school] and district people [who] were saying, "We want to offer these electives and this elective and then this elective and this," and I'm thinking am I the*

only one in the room who understands it? When you have a small school you can't offer a hundred electives. You've only got eighty sophomores. What are you going to do? Teach five different English classes? Eventually people realize it's about offering choices within the core as opposed to choices outside the core. Instead of offering five different English classes, offer kids in the same English class five different choices of how to learn and accomplish the same goals by reading different literature. If you give kids a choice of what literature to read in their regular English class and they can read black literature, then you aren't forced to offer an elective class to meet that need.

A large comprehensive school can provide a broad range of course offerings; a small school instead customizes its curriculum, providing a narrower range of courses but allowing more student choice within each course. Increased personalization within the small school is possible because teachers and students know each other well; they build from that knowledge to design courses and ensure that students master skills and content.

A school's curricular identity is not just a function of its academic curriculum—it is the whole of the school's offerings. Small schools can expand students' experiences in a variety of ways, including clubs, field trips, internships, or using *intercession*—where students intensively study elective courses over a short time period—as a strategy for adding more variety. For example, one goal of Boston's Fenway High School is to address issues related to race, class, gender, and other types of diversity. Of Fenway's 270 students, 49 percent are black, 25 percent Hispanic, and 22 percent white. Fenway addresses diversity and different perspectives through its academic curriculum, but also through its clubs, assemblies, and advisory system. Students at Fenway can join culture clubs whether or not they are members of that culture—the goal is exploration and understanding. Three to four times a year a club volunteers to present aspects of a group's culture, such as dances or poetry, to a whole-school assembly, and to convey for students that group's experience in their country of origin and in America. Within their advisory structure, students remain with a diverse group of classmates over their high school career, and many activities are devoted to understanding the perspective of others in the group. Through their advisory, Fenway students develop a deep understanding of perspectives from other cultures. Fenway is able to integrate its intellectual goals through multiple aspects of its school's design and practice.

Meanwhile, although large comprehensive high schools do offer a variety of electives, participation rates in these additional courses or extracurricular activities is relatively low (Monk, 1987; Schoggen & Schoggen, 1988).

Few students benefit from the variety of courses and activities that large high schools offer.

Advanced Placement Classes: Many Roads to Postsecondary Education

Many small schools are unable to offer the range of advanced placement courses that a large high school can, and this leads the school community to worry about how the school can prepare all students for college. Advanced placement courses appeal to many for three reasons:

- They are seen as the most challenging high school courses offered.

- They provide an advantage for competitive college admissions.

- They provide college credit, depending on the outcome of the Advanced Placement test.

Advanced placement courses are not an essential way of preparing students for postsecondary education. Schools have many alternative ways to ensure students are competitive in admissions, receive the academic and intellectual skills they need to succeed, experience other activities and develop skills that help them take advantage of the opportunities that present themselves when they are in college, and even help students earn college credit. However, as research has indicated, the dropout rate in large comprehensive high schools is high, and the college entrance rate is low. The change to new autonomous small schools is often predicated on the need to have high expectations for all students and to ensure that each student is prepared for postsecondary education. Autonomous small schools can prepare all students for postsecondary education through measures like these:

- Creating a rigorous core curriculum and eliminating electives that do not challenge students intellectually

- Offering other opportunities, such as internships, to help students develop a broader perspective on the world and learn to use their minds well

- Staging a senior exhibition or portfolio process that challenges students and allows them to demonstrate that they can work at high levels of mastery

- Creating a college placement program that allows individual high school students to enroll in college classes and earn dual credit

- Creating a Middle College High School, which gives a whole cohort of students an opportunity to earn their high school diploma while taking college classes and accruing college credit

In addition, if the staff of a small autonomous school decide that they believe advanced placement programs are a good means to develop students' intellectual skills, they can simply require that all students enroll in an advanced placement class. Alternatively, they can offer advanced placement classes across all schools (cross-over) and limit the problems to the schedule by scheduling these classes before or after school. They can also have students take the exam even if they did not enroll in an advanced placement course.

Advanced placement classes, or other programs such as International Baccalaureate, offer a curriculum with an external standard that is perceived as demanding. Offering such a curriculum to all students is a way to counter arguments that small schools will not prepare children for college or that they will not be as competitive for college admission. By requiring that everyone take this curriculum, everyone has access to the same demanding curriculum. Not everyone is required to take the final tests, but each student has been provided access to the curriculum (and, of course, other appropriate supports to succeed).

This is exactly what Clover Park High School, in Lakewood, Washington, has decided to do. Clover Park had offered pre-AP English classes and basic English classes to ninth and tenth graders. Essentially, the school was tracking students. Then, according to Paul Tytler, the school's principal, the school's leadership decided, "We're just not going to do that. If [Pre-AP] is our best curriculum, then this is the curriculum for every student." They have eliminated tracks and offer all students a high-quality education. This requires that previously homogeneous classes be mixed. The challenge for staff now is to learn how to differentiate instruction and work with students who traditionally have not been in more advanced courses (this challenge was previously discussed in Chapter Six).

What to Share: School Autonomy and Shared Resources

Autonomous small schools sharing the same building are often—especially during the conversion process—pushed to pool resources to offer more electives and activities than any school can provide alone. Table 8.1 shows the range of sharing options, with their advantages and drawbacks.

A common solution offered to the problem of offering fewer classes is to implement cross-over classes. A cross-over occurs when a student in one small school takes a class offering in another small school. The reasoning behind cross-over classes is that, if another school in the same building has a course that a student wants to take, then it follows that the student should have access to that course. While we have already discussed the

TABLE 8.1

Advantages and Drawbacks to Sharing Resources

Resource to Share	Advantages	Drawbacks
Classes	Students have a wider variety of electives	Cross-over classes reduce a school's autonomy (for example, over schedule and staffing) and cultural distinctness.
Other activities (band, sports, choir, clubs)	Students have a wider variety of choices.	Drawbacks are similar to those for classes, but less severe as these activities do not disrupt the instructional core of the schools.
Teachers	Students have a wider variety of choices within their school.	Teachers find it much more difficult to get to know students and personalize their education.
		Staff collaboration is also more difficult to arrange and maintain.

benefits and disadvantages of electives, cross-over courses pose some unique challenges.

The difficulty in allowing cross-over classes is that it affects the inner workings of the participating schools in a way that presents a lot of administrative strain. If a school has created its structure and culture—including its schedule and distinct sense of community—to meet its unique vision, then to allow cross-over the school will most likely have to change its schedule to ensure that all the classes in a building meet at the same time each day so that cross-over classes can occur. Each small school's schedule is based on its own needs, including when staff need to collaborate, when students engage in their internship opportunities, the provision of extended independent study time for students to prepare for their portfolio or end-of-year performance assessment, or the use of block schedules to extend learning, among other possibilities. The chance that several small schools will make all the same choices just because they share a physical plant is vanishingly remote. And changing a schedule to accommodate the needs of other schools plays havoc with all these interconnected parts—both for the schools offering access to classes and those whose students are invited to participate. Further, the personalized relationships and sense of belonging to a distinct community at the center of a small school culture are also affected.

Steve Shapiro, school change coach at Brookhaven High School in Columbus, Ohio, describes his approach to discussing cross-over classes:

Our goal is to just minimize [cross-overs] as much as we can. We know that the more shared staff we have, the more classes that involve students from more than one school that we have, the less autonomous the school's schedule's going to be, the less flexible they can be in terms of how they use their time. We've really worked—OK, you've got to have band, and if you're going to have one band and you can only have one band that's fine, but let's really intentionally reduce the number of places that we share students and share staff.

If a school has a focused curriculum based on a unified vision and philosophy, and if the school is staffed with the correct number of teachers for the number of students enrolled, then a school can realize its mission through its autonomies, personalized curriculum, and distinct school culture. As one teacher-leader turned small school principal said, "When you start to make exceptions [to autonomy], that's where you get into trouble." The trouble is that it minimizes the ability of teachers and students at one school to develop a strong, distinct culture, and limits their ability to know each other well.

Shael Suransky, principal of Bronx International High School, one of three small autonomous schools at the former Morris High School in New York City, discusses his school's approach to sharing resources. His school opened in 2001, accepting applicants for the ninth grade from recent immigrant students who needed support in developing language skills. The large comprehensive high school with which he shares a building is being phased out and has stopped accepted incoming ninth-grade students.

We share sports teams. The kids would prefer to have their own but we think it's a good idea to share because anything that doesn't touch the core operations and instructional structures of the school [helps you to] develop communities across schools; you just don't want that to affect the mission of the school negatively. The reason to create the small schools is to have autonomous faculties that know each other well and can move around a common vision, to create a community for kids where everyone's known well, and to create a manageable leadership position for the principal where they can really know each of their teachers well. For that you need to have distinct operational and instructional structures, but for extracurricular stuff like sports teams, clubs—we started a media project that goes across schools where kids published a magazine—those are good things to pool resources on and it's good to expose kids to other kids and you can get a lot of the advantages of a big school by sharing in those areas. Sometimes people want to push that border further to share special education and English as a second language services, for example, which on the surface makes sense because not everyone necessarily has that many. But I argue against that idea because I think it goes to the heart of the instructional program of a school—how you deal with your kids who [need the most support academically]. If that's something that's farmed out as a separate thing from each school into a common, central space it means no one's accountable for those kids in the schools. That's the standard that I use to think about sharing resources.

A common trade-off that has been occurring when the idea of cross-over classes has appeal to a large number of constituents is to limit such cross-overs to eleventh- and twelfth-grade students. In this way, ninth- and tenth-grade students have a chance to remain in their small school, become part of its culture, and develop strong relationships with other students and staff. Those who have made this compromise wonder if these students will want to take classes outside of their own school when the time comes. Some believe that, since cross-over classes reflect the belief that small schools might not serve students well, students who have experienced two years of small schools will not have any desire for cross-over classes, which will then be eliminated.

Two other trade-offs or solutions have been offered. First, some schools schedule the first or last period of the school day (or both) at the same time. Cross-over classes can occur during these periods and still allow the school to have the remainder of the day to use their schedule autonomy as they wish. Second, some schools offer these classes before or after school on a voluntary basis.

Concluding Thoughts

Rather than frame a discussion around what is gained or lost in the move to create small high schools from large ones, we pose a different question, paraphrasing Roellke (1996): What are the conditions that facilitate curricular effectiveness within all high schools? We suggest that two such conditions are a coherent vision-driven curriculum and personalized practice. These conditions provide the foundation from which small autonomous schools can develop creative ways to provide ongoing curriculum with both depth and breadth.

Chapter 9

Sharing the Building

CONVERTING A COMPREHENSIVE high school into multiple small autonomous schools typically means that the large building houses more than one new school. These schools are *interconnected*—that is, each shares a site with other school communities but has control over a contiguous space that it can call its own. Interconnected schools function most effectively when they come to agreements about how to work together, share facilities, and solve and negotiate issues that arise. Prosaic though they may seem, facility-sharing issues can affect the quality of the culture and the personalization of the environment each interconnected school can create.

Resources and physical space are central tools used to transform school culture and curricula. The sharing of limited resources and the unavoidable mixing of students and teachers in hallways and outside buildings means that interconnected schools will influence one another's climate and curricular strategies, as well as their ability to work toward new educational missions. In effect, they can all hinder or support their neighbors' ability to achieve their mission. Therefore, one of the most important aspects of sharing a building is developing the trusting relationships and communication that allow for setting common goals, making resources decisions, and resolving conflicts. The new neighbors need a way to be accountable to one another. George York, principal of Bronx High School for the Visual Arts, says: "When the students come in, they [need to] understand that, while they're a part of a different school, they're part of a larger school too and there are large building and smaller building needs. When it comes to common building concerns and needs—when I enter, when I exit, when I can use the facilities, when I can use the lunchroom—it really is keeping those lines of communication open and respect and learning to negotiate."

This chapter describes common issues that face interconnected schools and the ways that these schools have worked to create systems for dealing with these concerns.

Common Concerns

These are some of the issues and concerns that schools sharing the same building need to consider:

- School culture and contiguous space

- Decision-making structures

- Decision-making process (including a conflict resolution process)

- Shared expectations

- Shared services and facilities, including coordinating the schedules of shared space and deciding which resources to share in the name of fiscal efficiency (for example, using one janitorial service, or hiring one person to coordinate custodial needs for the whole building)

School Culture and Contiguous Space

The importance of creating a unique school culture cannot be minimized. The culture of a school permeates every aspect of its practices and environment and every aspect of practices and environment contributes to the culture. A school's space is an important element in creating a strong, safe, distinct culture. Creating a sense of place, culture, and purpose for learning is particularly important in interconnected schools. Such cultures share the following characteristics:

- The school environment feels definitively student-centered and owned, exhibiting a respect for and appreciation of youth culture.

- The physical environment looks clean and cared for.

- Signs of positive community identity (and a sense of belonging) permeate the school and the members of the school's community are happy to be a part of it.

- People feel a sense of responsibility to one another and to the larger school community, and they accept mutual accountability for their shared environment.

- The learning environment is both welcoming and relevant to students.

Visitors to interconnected schools should be able to feel when they have left one school and entered another. Schools can have signage over distinct entrances and exits, and aspects of interior design—including banners, paintings, and other wall decorations—can serve to differentiate schools and illuminate aspects of a school's culture. The school's classroom layout or use of other space is conducive to the vision of learning and teaching the school holds.

Decision-Making Structures

Almost every conversion team we spoke with has created some type of Building Council, and those that have not suffer from many internal problems. Typically, the principals who share a physical plant form a Building Council, with the idea that the small school principals need to make sure all the administrators communicate regularly, without fail. The Building Council is typically responsible for balancing the schools' individual autonomy with their need to coexist in shared space. It is a place where internal issues can be debated and discussed fairly, as well as one that presents a unified, and thus significant, voice to the larger community beyond the school.

Most Building Councils meet each week for two or three hours to look at whatever issues affect more than one school in the building. The Building Council is typically chaired by one of the principals, or the schools hire a building manager or facilitator. In either case, this person is responsible for facilitating weekly meetings, arranging shared resources, and being responsible for the larger building.

Some conversion efforts currently use or are considering using a site principal instead of a building manager to oversee the interconnected schools. In this scenario, the site principal has some authority to make decisions for each of the small schools. For example, one site principal would have veto power over the hires that each small school principal makes. The rationale for this central authority is that the small school principals are new to their positions, and would benefit from an experienced hand making some important decisions.

We argue against such a position for three reasons. First, placing authority for important school matters in a central facility-wide position undermines the autonomy of the new small school leaders and staff—those closest to the learner—to make the decisions that affect the learners. Second, appointing a facility principal has frequently resulted in many of the comprehensive school structures remaining in place, making it easier for the schools to backslide into comprehensive culture. Third, it implies that the district and conversion leaders do not fully trust or support the new small autonomous schools.

Who the building manager should be depends greatly on the skills, experiences, and needs of the small school directors. There are ways to provide and scaffold support to new school principals without undermining their autonomy and authority. Some schools have decided they needed a building manager who could advocate for their building with the district. Others decided that the principals could assume that advocacy role on a rotating basis. Another believes that the position would be expertly filled by the head custodian. In Chicago, for example, campus managers have no responsibilities for improving instruction. Instead, they work with small school principals to negotiate the use of space, supervise shared staff such as librarians and technology coordinators, and manage custodial, food, and security services for the building.

Because the duties involve negotiating relationships and resolving conflicts, it is important that this role be staffed by someone who has the needed skills and the respect of the schools and their stakeholders. A challenge in this role is that the incumbent is junior to all the principals and so has little formal authority. Often, the principal of the comprehensive high school has been suggested, but (as we discuss in Chapter Eight) this is not without its problems.

At Columbus High School in New York (which houses five small autonomous schools and one large comprehensive high school), Gerry Garfin, who had retired as principal of Columbus High School before the conversion, was hired to be the building adviser and manager. Garfin knew the building and had many years of experience within the district, while the small school principals were relatively new to their work. He could also use his experience to mentor the newer principals. Here's how he describes the way he approached his role: "It wasn't my job to go back and squeal on the principal who wasn't buying in. It was my job to talk to them and explain to them why it's important they buy in to what we were doing. . . . I think it's important that the building leader be a person who can swallow his ego, understand the greater picture, and is willing to act as a building facilitator." Garfin was able to provide effective support for the new principals without undermining their authority.

In one large high school that converted into five smaller schools, the new small school principals were the previous larger building principal, two assistant principals, and two new administrators not from the conversion school. The district asked that the previous large school principal be their sole contact at the building. However, this reinforced the large school aura. Instead, the five came together and decided what made sense for them. The two new administrators did not feel ready to handle this task on top of opening schools, so the group had the two previous assistant principals, who had some organizational management experience within the district, share the district liaison duties.

Decision-Making Process

Principals were nearly unanimous in agreeing that the decisions made about the use of the school building need to be made by the schools themselves. Having a superintendent who forces the schools to make their own decisions is a way to support the development of this relationship, and to create a consensus model for decision making. Further, the schools should want to make those decisions that affect them rather than to let an outside agent do so. As George York says, "We knew that we had to solve it for ourselves because if anything is imposed from outside we would react. Our whole sense is that [they should] tell us what we need to do, what's required, and we will solve it to our satisfaction."

Shael Suransky, principal of Bronx International High School, gives an example of a negotiation that occurred in his building:

> One school this summer decided they wanted to change their time for lunch, which affected everyone else, and it was at the last minute and so was not something people were happy about. They first had to convince us to consider it, and then once they did we had to come up with a plan that satisfied them and everyone else and it's not always going to be an equitable solution. Someone's going to win sometimes. But it's getting everyone to a point where they win sometimes and you have a consensus that is a working consensus.

Schools have used consensus rather than one-person-one-vote decision making because, as Suransky says, "I think [one-person-one-vote] can work if you're OK with people losing completely, which, to me, doesn't make a lot of sense. I think it's about raising the bar where everyone has to be willing to let this move forward even if they're not totally happy. Think about consensus decision making in terms of sufficient consensus—which is different from "I love this." It's more like "OK, I can live with this."

The consensus approach works through negotiation and often requires facilitation within the Building Council to ensure that everyone's position emerges and people move beyond their initial positions to figure out a solution that is acceptable to everyone. Usually when conflict arises, it doesn't engage all the schools at once, so often the other principals can play a mediating role and provide guidance.

Gerry Garfin describes the negotiating process in these terms:

Principals have to swallow their ego and say, "You know something, we're all in the same building for one purpose, to educate kids whether they're my kids or someone else's kids. They're all kids in the same building and they're all entitled to the same quality education, they're all entitled to the use of all facilities and it's not mine versus yours. It's all of ours." And there has to be a meeting of the minds. . . . That's tough when egos get involved but people have to give in to the needs of the entire building as compared to the needs and interests of one specific school. . . . "It's not what we wanted, but because of the greater need of all the kids we will change what we're doing."

Shared Expectations

High-functioning interconnected schools develop a set of common expectations around hallway noise level, skipping classes, attendance, and tardiness because those issues affect the climate, sense of space, and the ability to shape relationships at every school. When students are not in class or are loud as they move through the halls, it affects all students and staff. Having a shared set of rules and expectations means that students will be treated fairly by all schools. Each school wants to ensure that its students are treated well by the other schools, that its rules are respected by the other schools, and that its efforts to create a new culture are not undermined. Creating shared expectations around discipline has consistently emerged as a challenge across interconnected schools. Schools often have different expectations and different ways of handling discipline. This is particularly true where small schools and large schools share the same building. If schools are diligent and work hard to create conflict resolution, however, eventually it will not be a concern.

No matter how separate the facilities, students will interact with students from other schools, and behavioral problems will occur. Many incidents occur because it is easier for students to engage in a conflict with someone outside their immediate community. Schools can shift the students' sense of community to view the larger facility as a community to which they also belong. Suransky argues:

Whenever there's a conflict across schools we make a much bigger deal about it with the kids than if it's internal. For example, there's an automatic suspension of kids if there's actually a fight. We usually make it a longer suspension because it's across schools and when we can't do an effective conflict resolution with the kids we bring in the families. Usually those conflict resolutions are done by principals as opposed to guidance counselors or deans; again, to stress its importance and significance.

A fundamental challenge for interconnected schools is to establish ways to hold each other accountable for shared expectations. For example, schools might share the same standard minimum level of attendance, but one school may have difficulty in meeting that level. Because they share a site, one school's truancy equals disruption for the other schools. Having an effectively facilitated Building Council is important for schools to be able to have difficult conversations of how they will hold each other accountable.

Shared Services and Facilities

Interconnected schools most commonly share the library, computer rooms, physical education facilities, lunch facilities, sports teams, band, and security, which includes school entrances. Schools also make decisions on the use of the school building after hours, for evening or weekend programs and activities. The building manager typically is responsible for keeping a master facility schedule. Interconnected small schools can share custodial or repair services, which can also be organized by the building manager.

Sharing space is possible, and contributes to a building-wide culture of sharing and communication. Sharing space in a facility is also one of the most challenging aspects for interconnected schools. The principals we spoke with believed that interconnected schools need to reach an understanding and a respect that they are all in it together and have to learn to work together, because each school is giving up a little space and getting a little space. None believed that it was an ideal situation, in that schools are not going to get all the rooms and all the facilities they want. Of course, very few stand-alone schools really ever feel they have enough space either. In many cases, schools have teachers sharing rooms, and this is no different.

Other Challenges

Space constraints, especially in densely populated cities such as New York, have dictated that some new small schools will be housed in buildings with large comprehensive high schools that have no plans to convert. This is a particularly challenging setting in which to create a new, different culture of teaching and learning—and such cases demand extraordinary efforts on the part of both the small school and the comprehensive school to give the small school the space it needs to develop its own identity. That the large school serves a majority of the building's students, even if several small schools also occupy space in the building, raises issues of equity. For example, if the large school serves twenty-five hundred students, and three small schools serve three hundred students each, are decisions weighted so that each school has an equal say, or weighted to the majority of students? In other situations, small schools share a building with a large school that is phasing itself out. In these situations, having a well-developed Building Council, where challenging issues can be discussed and negotiated, is vital to the healthy functioning of each school.

Concluding Thoughts

Sharing a building is not easy, but the principals we spoke with believe that doing so can greatly benefit each small school. Each multiplex, like each small school, will choose an approach that works best for its needs, but multiplexes in general have a set of common needs: establish a commitment to shared, equitable use; build and maintain strong, trusting relationships; develop a conflict resolution process; and support the ability of each school to create its unique culture. We hope that having a chance to deliberate on these key needs will help interconnected schools create the governance structure that best suits their communities.

Part 3

Transition Planning

Chapter 10

Roll-Out Plans for New Autonomous Small Schools

THE DECISION TO TRANSFORM comprehensive high schools can create a sense of urgency to get the job done quickly. For those of us who believe that small schools make a huge difference in the lives of students, the current system is failing. But in most communities, people feel attached to many elements of the old large school—the name, the teams, the building, the sense of history in the halls. So while some may feel tremendous energy for change, many—including some who do see the need for smaller schools—also feel a strong gravitational pull to keep things the same, to move slowly, to tinker. We take it as a premise that despite the pull to go slowly, to make only small changes, it makes sense to move as decisively as possible toward full-fledged small autonomous schools.

Just how to *roll out,* or phase, the opening of new small schools involves a number of design decisions, including these: the total intended number of new schools, their size, and when and with which grades they will open. In this chapter, we examine these decision points, describing options and trade-offs and providing examples of a variety of plans that have been tried. Rather than advocating a specific roll-out plan, we urge each school and district to devise a plan that takes into account the local context and these guiding questions:

- How do we decisively interrupt current practice and culture so as to transform our schools and district to meet our new shared vision?

- How can we create new small schools most effectively and quickly?

- How will we establish cultures of high expectations in our new schools?

- How should we phase in our new district and school organizational structure?

- What will happen to students who are currently in our large high school and those in the feeder schools? How can we do an effective job of serving any students remaining in the old school as we launch the new ones?

- What is our ability to support educators' capacity to function in these new environments and how does this affect our roll-out decisions?

- How will roll-out plans develop or hinder ownership from the different stakeholder groups in our community?

Key Decision Points

Schools have used a variety of roll-out plans for opening their new small autonomous schools. Some have created distinct 9–12 schools in one year (the big bang), while others have gradually phased in the new autonomous small schools over a number of years, moving school by school, grade by grade, or some combination of both. Some efforts have had all the schools start in the same building, while others have been *hothoused,* that is, the new school was opened in a different location, allowed to establish its unique culture and practice, and then moved back to the older building to join other new small schools. Others have created small learning communities or academies as a step in the process toward autonomous schools.

All converting schools and their districts must grapple with the following six issues:

- The *timing* of school openings. Options:

  New schools open simultaneously.

  New schools open sequentially.

- The *location* of the schools. Options:

  Co-housing: All the schools are housed in the same building or campus.

  Hothousing: One or more of the schools is created in a separate location and then brought back to the main building.

  Seeding: A successfully operating small school is brought into the main building to provide an example and serve as a mentor to the new schools.

  Multi-level: The schools are opened in a building shared with preschools, elementary schools, or middle schools.

  Carve-out: One or more new small schools is housed in a building with a large comprehensive school (which may or may not have plans for conversion).

- The *grade levels* served at opening. Options:

  Open for Grades 9–12.

  Open for Grade 9, or Grades 9 and 10.

  Open with other combinations, including lower grades, with the intention of creating a K–12 school.

- *Student access* within the district. Options:

  Students from the converting school must stay with one of the new schools being created from that school.

  Students can enroll in any of the array of options in the district. For example, students from one converting school can move to a new small school that was created from a different converting school (or to another comprehensive high school in the district).

- *School size.* Options:

  All the new small schools serve the same number of students.

  Different small schools serve different numbers of students.

- *Preparatory structures.* Options:

  Move directly to full-fledged small schools.

  Start with alternate preparatory stages such as "small learning communities," "academies," "sheltered schools," or other programs targeted at specific segments of the student body.

All the options for these six decision points have both pitfalls and strengths. In the following sections, we discuss these issues, drawing on experiences of our colleagues around the country.

The Timing of School Openings

Some conversion design teams have decided to open their new small schools all at once (affectionately known as the "big bang" approach); others use a phased approach, opening new schools over two to three years. In either case, the goal is to provide the greatest chance of creating successful, sustainable small schools while offering the best education to the most students as quickly as possible. We also must note that saying "big bang" or "all at once" is somewhat misleading. Even when a comprehensive school breaks into new schools on one big day, this generally happens in schools and communities that have already undergone significant dialogue about why a change is necessary and what change is best. In most cases, the discussion has taken at least a couple of years before the new schools actually open.

The decision regarding how quickly to move forward depends largely on the school community's readiness for the change, the ability of the school or district to move forward, and the reasons for making the change in the first place. Max Silverman, principal of Tyee High School, believes that schools should get small as quickly as possible because that makes it easier to focus on instructional practice. Marcy Raymond, senior program officer in school improvement at KnowledgeWorks, believes that school communities that do a thorough self-analysis and create a strategic plan based on their analysis thereby develop a deep understanding of why they are making the change and of the weaknesses of the school as it currently exists. The process of self-analysis also gives school communities the skills they need to handle a fast-paced conversion effort—while continuing to remain reflective and adaptable when problems arise. For Raymond, the motivation for the conversion is a central element in determining the speed of the conversion effort. For example, schools that are explicitly tracked or that have differences in course matriculation based upon socioeconomic or racial factors have a strong impetus to convert quickly, seeking to redress such inequities as quickly as possible.

Big Bang

Thus the big bang approach offers the advantage that the goal of providing all students with a small school is realized quickly. None of the current students are left behind in poorly performing large schools, and none of the current upperclassmen find themselves staying in a school that is being phased out, which tends to be a depressing environment. At the same time, such a sudden change can be disorienting to everyone involved, which is enough in itself to make some want to drag their feet. And if some stakeholders are not fully convinced of the need and ready for the change, the process will be made even more difficult by their temptation to welcome delays.

Phased Approach

Phasing allows subsequent school starts to build on the learning from the experience of the earliest schools to open. They face fewer surprises, and they tend to get up and running more easily as a result. But they may be required to function without the best example, as the first schools to open must establish their new practices within the context of the larger school, whose culture can undermine a shift to more effective teaching and learning. In addition, new small schools that open in the midst of an ongoing comprehensive school may find their autonomy restricted because of needs and structures of the larger school.

The Location of the Schools

Regarding where to locate the new small schools, some schools and districts have little choice: they have nowhere else to house a small school and no other small schools to bring into their large school building. These districts typically open all their new small schools in the building that originally housed the comprehensive high school.

For those districts that have other buildings and schools, hothousing and seeding offer potential advantages. Hothousing, whereby a small school is started in a separate location and then brought to a different, usually larger, school building, gives a new small school a chance to develop its own culture without the influence of the larger school. The process resembles that of creating a start-up stand-alone school. Later, when the school has developed strength of purpose and a sustainable school culture, it is brought back to the larger school. Sometimes a decision is ultimately made for the school to remain in its current location. The best-known example of hothousing is the Julia Richman Complex (JREC) in New York. Though unique in many ways, JREC has proven to be a powerful and compelling model of exemplary schooling.

Seeding, or bringing an established school into the mix of new small schools in a multiplex, has other advantages. The staff and student body of the seed school, experienced with small school dynamics and operations, can provide ready on-site mentoring and brainstorming, both informal and formal, for the people in the converting school. The presence and vitality of a strong small school can also help show the comprehensive school community what can be gained and allay concerns about what is lost in the process of converting to a small school.

In the current push to convert comprehensive high schools, districts tend to focus exclusively on high schools, rather than seeking to incorporate other levels in the mix at any given school site. But approaches that group different levels of schools together deserve consideration. Educators at JREC, which includes six schools, argue that the addition of middle and elementary school students changes the old high school culture and reinvigorates staff and students alike. They find that the youngest students, in particular, are a positive influence on the behavior of older students, and the multi-age population gives the school building the feel of a community.

Space constraints often mean that new small schools must share space with comprehensive high schools that have no plans to convert. As discussed in Chapter Nine, it is particularly challenging to develop an effective small school culture while sharing a building with a comprehensive school that intends to keep its current structure, and success requires sincere effort on the part of both schools.

Co-Housing

When the old comprehensive school is broken up into smaller units that are all starting out together, the new school teams can work with and learn from one another. Meanwhile, all students and teachers have access to the original school facilities—gym, athletic fields, auditorium, or whatever it had. However, it is often difficult to make the fact of the change tangible— the same staff and students still show up at the same location each morning, and the old culture may seem to linger in the air and physical environment.

Hothousing

Setting the initial operations up in a separate location establishes a new autonomous small school decisively. No one can have any doubt that they're not doing business as usual, and the new school can create its own culture and instruction without interference from established patterns. Of course, you first have to find (and pay for) a stand-alone location suitable for the new school.

When it works, hothousing can work very well indeed. For example, Skyview High School, a part of Mapleton Public Schools (the district introduced in Chapter Two), is using a phased roll-out approach and plans to hothouse two or more of its currently planned six autonomous small schools. In fall 2004, Skyview opened two small schools on separate campuses; it plans to open four more schools in fall 2005 on the main campus. Skyview believes that hothousing will provide these early schools with the chance to develop their own identity and culture. Housing the schools elsewhere also allows for renovations at the main campus, which will accommodate multiple autonomous small schools in the future. Skyview's first two spin-off schools will be hothoused for two years to allow them to develop their own identity and then they will probably be brought back to the large multiplex. The two hothouse schools will each open with 120 students, split between Grades 9 and 10. When they return to the main campus in 2006, they will join four schools of 400 students apiece that have been co-housed there.

Seeding

Seeding provides an established school to serve as an exemplar for new small schools. The experience and atmosphere of the seed school can be a powerful resource for those new to small schools, showing them what practices of small autonomous schools look like and can be. Unfortunately, such small schools are hard to come by; few districts have them on tap. Further, the move into quarters shared by students and staff who are still accustomed to the culture of a comprehensive school inevitably causes disruption for the seed school.

The difficulties can be overcome, however. Located in the Bronx, Christopher Columbus High School houses six thousand students. In 2001, Columbus launched the Pelham Preparatory Academy, a program consisting of a project director and a hundred Christopher Columbus students. In New York, a *program* functions as a sheltered school. That is, it has all the autonomy that small schools need, including budget autonomy, but is officially part of a larger school. This allows the school to develop with some protection provided by the larger school. In 2002, the program transformed itself into a new small school and was joined in the building by another new autonomous small school, the Bronx Academy of Visual Arts. In 2003, another autonomous school—Global Enterprise Academy—joined the mix along with two new programs, which each became autonomous schools in 2004. Of the five small schools sharing the building with Columbus High School in 2004–2005, the two schools brought in from outside have principals, staff, and students mainly from outside Columbus. The three schools developed as programs were founded with staff and students originally from Columbus. This seeding of a school with experienced small school staff was one way to pave the way for successful small school conversion. All the schools and programs started with ninth graders and built up from there.

Multi-Level

A multi-level building, where the small autonomous high school shares the space with schools of other grade levels, turns out to be a remarkably effective environment. Having students of different ages in the same building decisively disrupts current practice and facilitates transformation of culture. For example, observers report that older students often act more mature around younger students than they do when left to their own devices. In addition, the school can staff more fully as a community building. Of course, it's difficult to find space for all the new small high schools the district needs while accommodating the younger students as well. The elementary school community also tends to feel somewhat uncomfortable about having young students mix with high school students; the cultural influences can go both ways, and not all the high schoolers will display the maturity to be a good influence.

Carve-Out

It can seem like an easy shortcut to simply have the new small school share space with a large comprehensive high school. This arrangement offers the physical advantages of co-housing, allowing the small school to use facilities typically found in larger schools. But it is difficult to transform practices and establish a thriving new school culture in the shadow of a less-healthy one, especially one that doesn't expect to reap the benefits of conversion for itself.

The Grade Levels Served at Opening

Which grade levels will the new small schools serve when they open? Most schools have opened with either a full 9–12 school or with Grade 9 or Grades 9 and 10 only, though there are exceptions to this. One such exception is School of the Arts High School in Chicago. School of the Arts High School was designed by a group of the comprehensive school's ninth-grade teachers, and these teachers wanted to launch their school with students they knew well—so they began the school with tenth-grade students only, and then expanded in both directions.

Opening with Grades 9–12 has obvious advantages: it provides the whole student body with the excitement and energy of being part of a new school, rather than ensuring that some current students will miss the opportunity to participate in a positive change. Also, opening all the new schools for the whole high school population at the same time means that the new schools will not have to coexist with a school that is phasing out an old, often negative culture. Unfortunately, as some of our colleagues have found, it can be hard to incorporate upperclassmen into a new kind of school: they've already learned the ropes of the big school, and they do not necessarily welcome the change. A number of teams have sought to avoid this pitfall by involving students on the design teams, helping to nurture students' sense of dedication to and ownership of the new schools. (Nurturing student commitment and ownership is discussed more fully in Chapter Four.)

Many school design teams have decided to begin with just the ninth grade, believing that by serving students who have never been in high school before, the schools can create their own culture and identity without being influenced by the negative atmosphere of the big school. Ninth graders do not have the experience of high school, or the experience of changing what they are used to. Their high school experience can be defined as a small school experience from the beginning.

Maureen Benson, principal of Youth Empowerment School (YES) Academy in Oakland, California, thought that beginning with ninth and tenth grades would be beneficial, even though the tenth graders had not participated in an academy. By including tenth graders, the new school would have students who remembered the larger high school. They would be in a position to assure the ninth graders that the small school was better, so that the new students wouldn't feel they were missing out on what might have seemed to them to be exciting features of a comprehensive school.

Launching a new school after having created an academy at the old school can provide support for opening a new school with more than just ninth graders. Brookhaven, in Columbus, Ohio, created a ninth-grade academy while it was designing its conversion. The students from the academy, tenth graders when Brookhaven's new small schools were launched, were familiar with the small school concept through their experience in the academy; thus Brookhaven opened its schools with both ninth and tenth graders. We have found some reason to worry that creating academies sometimes slows down the process toward full conversion. In this case, however, developing the academy during the design year, with full intention to complete the process, seems to have strengthened and expedited the conversion.

Student Access Within the District

In general, districts approach conversion in two ways: on a school-by-school basis or on a multi-school or district-wide basis.

School by School

Districts that approach conversions on a school-by-school basis have viewed each school as responsible for shaping the conversion. In general, the staff and students at the given school building will be the same staff and students at that school building when the conversion process is completed. If all the schools in a district are converting, students and staff still remain in their original schools. If only some of the schools are converting, a few districts allow some teachers and students to transfer to and from nonconverting schools.

Conceptually, the school-by-school approach seems easier to manage. The logistics are certainly simpler. However, students have fewer options and may miss out on a school in another conversion that might be ideally suited to their interests or needs. Also, it is more difficult to change culture and instructional practice because all the same teachers and students remain together—they don't mix in new combinations likely to promote a culture-shift.

Cross-School

Some districts have viewed their conversions as cross-school. This approach typically involves a Request for Proposals (RFP) process by which any group of teachers or administrators—from the same or different schools—can come together and submit a proposal to create a new small school. In this context, teachers and administrators can join together based on a shared vision of schooling rather than out of the happenstance that they currently work in the same building. In the Bronx in New York City, such RFP schools are then housed within various large school buildings in the city, sometimes in the school of origin (if some teachers do come from the same school), sometimes not. Although logistically more challenging than the school-by-school approach, allowing teachers and administrators from different buildings to create a small school brings together people who share similar beliefs regarding how students learn, which allows them to share and develop practice collegially and often means they bring more enthusiasm to the effort.

Of the two comprehensive high schools in Columbus, Ohio, one, Brookhaven, is converting immediately into three small schools; the other is planning on doing so a year later. Brookhaven, supported by the teachers union, has opened all of its small school positions to all teachers and plans to open the schools to all students in the district starting with the second class. Current teachers at Brookhaven have priority in filling positions in the new small schools located in the Brookhaven building, and then the positions will be filled according to the normal district procedure. Teachers at Brookhaven who do not want to teach in a small school are given "super seniority" in applying for openings at other district schools. The district and union do not believe any jobs will be lost in the process. Their maxim: "Nobody has a job with any school, one has a job with the district." All the new small schools opened with ninth and tenth grade. Ninth-grade students—the ones who would be tenth graders at the opening—chose among the new schools located in the Brookhaven building; eighth-grade students chose using the district's open enrollment process.

We recommend that districts engaged in conversion discussions consider taking this opportunity to revisualize and transform the district as a whole. Could a small autonomous high school be placed in an underutilized elementary school building? Could a middle school divide into multiple schools and one locate in a building that had previously housed the large high school? In many districts in which high schools have been converting, middle schools have also begun to raise the question of conversion. Thinking about conversion across all the schools in the district provides more options for students, and more options for schools and districts trying to establish positive cultures in their schools. As seen in the experience of the Julia Richman complex, younger students bring a community ethic to a large building, bringing out the nurturing, caring side of adolescents. Further, the creation of community organizations in a multiplex, like the health center at Julia Richman, can support the students as well as extending the school's reach and community into the surrounding neighborhood.

School Size

The Bill & Melinda Gates Foundation, which is funding much of the school conversion work currently taking place around the country, has set at four hundred the number of students a school can serve effectively and provide a personalized, intellectually vibrant experience. Research by the Small Schools Project in Washington has found that many schools have decided to break down into equal units with approximately four hundred students each (Lear, 2004).

We have some concern about the correlation between the guidelines of the Gates Foundation grants and the size of most conversion schools. One might expect that school sizes would vary widely, depending on the particular vision of each individual school and the needs of the diverse student populations. The sight of most schools' landing right around four hundred makes us wonder whether some conversion schools may not be engaging in conversations about ideal size that follow from a student-centered school vision, but instead letting factors such as the terms of a grant or insufficient time for consideration of a comprehensive system of small schools drive their decisions. While four hundred might be an ideal number for many schools—and it is certainly an improvement over the size of most current comprehensive schools—we urge conversion and design teams to base their school size choice, like all major design decisions, on their unique vision and their assessment of the range of student needs.

Some schools may choose a smaller (or larger) size because, for example, it supports their intent to create stronger relationships between teachers and students, to support a highly experiential curricular approach, to foster student choice over curriculum, or to meet the needs of a variety of student learning styles. Based on different priorities established at each of the new schools, the two high schools in West Clermont, Ohio, serving twenty-five hundred students, have converted into ten schools ranging in size from one hundred to four hundred students.

Lear reports that many of the schools that work with the Small Schools Project have in fact shifted their thinking about size. Many four-hundred-student schools find that the draw of trying to act like a comprehensive high school remains very strong, so they are contemplating becoming smaller. The smaller the school, typically the clearer the focus and the easier it is to hold to and organize around that philosophical focus. A school with 150 students and a staff of eight is unlikely to fall into the comprehensive high school trap—it just does not have the resources to be comprehensive and must set its priorities based on its vision.

For example, according to Sharon Brown, coach of Shaw High School in East Cleveland, Ohio, their conversation began with the knowledge that their new schools could be no larger than four hundred. Once the conversation started, staff began to discuss who their students were and what they needed. "Our kids are coming with significant deficits," or "We're really behind the game. . . . Maybe smaller is better for us." That's when we decided, "If four hundred is good, two hundred would be better. Let's go real small and build from there."

To take another example, Foster High School—an eight-hundred-student school located in Tukwila, Washington—serves a population that is 42 percent white, 24 percent black, and 16 percent each Asian and Hispanic, and 50 percent of all students are eligible for free and reduced-price lunch and 24 percent are considered English language learners. The school initially offered four academies of different sizes, all driven by curricular approaches. A brochure distributed by the school described them as follows:

> Experience Academy, *100 students, is ideal for students who prefer to learn by doing and want to study challenging curriculum that connects to the world. It involves field trips, internships, and job shadows.*
>
> Choices Preparatory Academy, *150 students, is ideal for students who like to have a voice in their own learning and benefit from working in a group to solve problems. This school would have classes collaboratively designed by teachers, students, and parents, and short, intensive courses.*
>
> Discovery Academy, *270 students, for students who like to study curriculum through a focused question and to explore content areas before going into a topic with greater depth. It involves a yearly curriculum focused around increasingly deeper essential questions.*
>
> Arts Academy, *270 students, for students who enjoy using the arts as a lens to explore other curriculum areas. It involves creating a portfolio, evening course options, internships, and integrated arts and academics.*

In this model, the student enrollment of each of the choices was driven by curricular approach. Because of low student interest, Choices Preparatory Academy did not become one of the final schools. Each of the new academies was able to accommodate the remaining teachers and students, taking more students than originally intended but being able to do so within its curricular approach with the addition of the teachers from the Choices Preparatory Academy.

Optional Preparation Structures

Some schools create small learning communities (SLCs) or academies as a step in the process of becoming a small school. This is an attempt to ease staff and students into the feel of small school and develop a staff's capacity for a more collaborative environment while retaining some of the structures of the larger school.

Daniel Baron, co-director of the National School Reform Faculty, located at the Harmony School in Bloomington, Indiana, believes that schools with the strongest SLCs will make the strongest small schools. He believes that schools that have the leadership and the focus to successfully convert to small learning communities are able to make the next transition to small schools. The benefit to using a SLC approach is that it provides time for school staff to become accustomed to smallness. Baron observes that the strongest SLCs realize that they would be more effective if they had more autonomy to meet their students' unique needs.

A cautionary note: Without strong support (district, community, and school-based) that ensures that this transitional structure will open as an autonomous school the next year, people are tempted to continue asking, "Why do we really want small schools?" Stakeholders can become convinced that tweaking the school through the small learning communities will resolve the challenges of the larger school. As we noted in Chapter One, while the changes are real and most likely result in increased personalization, SLCs and similar structures lack the autonomy they need to fully realize the benefits of smallness. It can be useful to move to a structure such as a "sheltered school" or a "program" at once, which can function almost entirely as an autonomous small school while preparing the school community for eventual full independence.

For example, the Pablo Neruda Academy for Architecture and World Studies began as a program with Lehman High School in 2003. As a program, Pablo Neruda was fairly autonomous in key ways. It had its own students and set its own policies. Its faculty and students had the latitude to create their own school culture. While Pablo Neruda's budget was administered by the larger school, its faculty administered all grants that they received. Faculty at Pablo Neruda were responsible both for reporting their students' attendance and for calling their parents. In its program year, Pablo Neruda was limited to drawing its students from the larger high school, but as an autonomous school, it became open to all students in the district. And Pablo Neruda now uses only the gym of the larger school—students registered in the small school have no cross-over courses at all. Starting as a program was "really a launching pad for becoming our school," says Dina Heisler, director.

Concluding Thoughts

While there is no one correct way to roll out a high school conversion, teams do encounter a set of predictable decision points. Each of these decision points provides the opportunity to set a context for reinvention and the launch of new schools that have the greatest chance of developing into fully autonomous, high-functioning schools. Each of the decision points provides a moment to weigh the value of moving fast against the value of taking time to lay the groundwork for change; to weigh giving teachers and students choice about where they will work against the demands of balance and equity; to weigh efficiencies of size and location. We hope that having a chance to deliberate on these decision points early in the process will help conversion schools make the choices that best suit their communities.

Chapter 11

Student Choice Options

NEW SMALL SCHOOLS are based on the idea that diverse learning environments and strategies are necessary for all students to succeed. Following the principle that no one school fits all students, the creation of a comprehensive system of new small autonomous schools provides an essential array of quality educational options. From this perspective, creating many new high schools, each with a unique mission and vision, provides choices about desired learning environments for students and their families. However, creating options does not in itself guarantee that all students will know about and select schools where they will receive the intellectual challenge they need to acquire the skills to succeed. New schools are created within an existing community and system, often one in which long-term inequities and patterns of social segregation and educational tracking exist. Conversion schools must strike a balance between student choice and the equitable distribution of student populations. This chapter describes the trade-offs of different policy options.

Choice and Equity

Districts need a policy to ensure that the new small schools do not become another sorting mechanism. A student assignment policy that balances the needs for choice and equity is vital in this regard. Lili Allen and Adria Sternberg of Jobs for the Future have written of two particular challenges for districts to be aware of when creating their policy (2004): avoiding interschool tracking and ensuring that all schools have high expectations of their students.

The Possibility of Creating a System of Tracked Schools

In a choice-based system of schools, it is likely that some parents have better access than others to information about schools and school staff or a better understanding of how to work the system to ensure that their child is enrolled in a particular school. Large comprehensive high schools are full of tracked classes—that is, classes specifically for students who are perceived to be performing at different achievement levels. This situation could easily be mirrored at the district level, with some schools populated by the former honors students and others by the general track students.

Ensure High Expectations in Each New School

Educators engaged in conversion have found that the type of vision a school offers has a large impact on student preference. Choosing career themes means that students might select their schools based on the public's perception of who has these jobs or vocations. For example, it might not be surprising that a school of computers and technology might be more heavily chosen by males; in turn, females will be overrepresented in other schools. It is never just one school that is unequal.

Further, if the career theme was based on a preexisting vocational or academic program, students may choose based upon the past perception of which kids that program served. For example, a business program with the reputation of being for the general noncollege track will not attract students from outside that track. This results in an inequitable distribution of students in the new school, since tracking has historically sorted low-income students and students of color in the lower, less challenging, non–college-ready tracks.

Trade-Offs in Student Assignment Policies

According to the year two evaluation report of the Bill & Melinda Gates Foundation Small Schools Program (American Institutes for Research & SRI International, 2004):

> Subdividing the student population of a large high school, especially when done entirely on the basis of student choice, poses the potential risk of fostering segregation by achievement level or race/ethnicity. Converting schools need to develop procedures for balancing students' preferences with the goal of obtaining diverse student bodies within each of the small schools or learning communities created through the conversion.

We have found schools using three main methods for student assignment: controlled choice, open choice, and the current district process (where policy exists). One other option that we saw involved schools that "got small," that is, large schools that converted to small autonomous schools without creating specific identities. In the get-small scenario, all teachers and students were assigned randomly, with equitable limits on the distribution of students in areas such as race, socioeconomic status, sex, and special needs. The rationale was that because the schools were alike, no one school should be more highly sought after. The main trade-off between partially controlled and fully open choice sets the district's ability to balance student population levels and ensure a mix at each school against the greater student and community enthusiasm likely to be generated by a fully free choice of school. The get-small approach sacrifices all the benefits of choice in the name of equity, hoping that the natural advantages of smallness and autonomy will develop the conditions and identity to generate enthusiasm and support after the schools open.

The Small Schools Project (2003b) lists the following questions to consider for student placement:

- How does the placement method we choose reflect our overall philosophy and values?

- Can we clearly articulate the rationale behind this placement method?

- Is it important to us that each of our small schools reflect the demographics of our larger school?

- If not, how much and what kinds of differences in terms of student demographics are we willing to accept in our small schools?

- How will we communicate student placement results to students and their parents?

- What are we doing to ensure that all our schools are attractive to students?

- If we are using balancing criteria, will some be more important than others?

- What do we want our application to include and why?

- Do we want to set maximum and minimum numbers of applications? If so, what steps will we take if a small school doesn't receive a minimum number of applications? If a small school receives too many?

- What steps will we take for those students who don't complete an application?

- Who will be involved in the sorting process and why?

- Have we set up fair and transparent application and sorting processes that our administrators can clearly articulate and defend if an appeal occurs?

In addition, another issue that confronts districts with more than one comprehensive high school is which of the new schools each student can choose to attend, as discussed in Chapter Ten. All districts allow incoming students to select from any new school. Current high school students are sometimes restricted in their choices. Some districts allow current high school students to choose only from new schools within their previous large comprehensive high school. Other districts have allowed for choice of any new small school in the district by any student.

The *National School District and Network Grants Program: Year 2 Evaluation Report* presents a research perspective on the questions of student choice and equity:

> *The task of student selection or assignment to small schools brings into play questions of how to meet students' needs and desires for a particular curricular emphasis and teaching approach while also achieving both racial/ethnic and ability-level diversity within each of the smaller units. Students and parents at some conversion schools cite a lowering of academic standards and express concern about access to fewer high level courses.*
>
> *In one sense, this equity issue ties back to that of teaching and learning. The lack of a clear, compelling demonstration that higher-achieving students can be challenged and well taught in diverse classrooms leaves the schools vulnerable to criticism from parents and the students themselves. Until teachers are adept at reaching all parts of the achievement distribution within the same classroom, many students and parents are likely to press for the old system of separate classes for high achievers. To provide guidance around achieving equity as well as addressing other challenges, reformers working on school conversion see a great need for a successful "model conversion," both to prove the viability of the conversion strategy and to provide specific guidance in the way that model small schools have done for start-up schools [American Institutes for Research & SRI International, 2004, p. 10].*

We do not promote open choice as a viable policy option; the probability that it will lead to inequitable enrollments is too high. For example, Manual High School in Denver, Colorado, one of the first large high schools to convert to small autonomous schools, began with an open choice policy. Unrestricted choice resulted in new schools that were severely imbalanced racially, leading to concerns that the schools were, in effect, tracking students.

In controlled choice, schools explicitly decide to allocate students, if necessary, to ensure that each school is relatively similar demographically—

that is, in areas such as race, sex, special education, English language ability, achievement, and income status. Each small school, then, represents the diversity of the district. This prevents some schools from *creaming,* that is, enrolling only the high-achieving students, and creates a diverse community where different perspectives can be shared. In this system, students typically rank their first three choices. The New England Small Schools Network, housed at the Center for Collaborative Education in Boston, believes that new small schools should be demographically similar within a range of plus or minus 5 percent. (For example, if 45 percent of students in a district are African American, then 40–50 percent of each school population would be African American students.) Of course, these policies have exceptions. Schools such as Manhattan or Bronx International High School are developed especially for students with specific language needs. Such schools should be allowed to enroll these students, students who have traditionally been underserved by large comprehensive high schools.

Some schools use what we call a modified controlled choice, which functions very similarly to an open choice system in practice. While school staff are cognizant of the danger that assignment only by student preferences can lead to inequitable distributions of students among the schools, their districts are relatively homogeneous and the major concern is gender equity. These schools don't abandon principles of equity—in fact, the schools are aware of them and will compare the new small schools based on student demographics. They often state that a guide to assignment will be demographics. These schools, however, do not explicitly state any demographic quotas at the beginning of the process, nor do they have any explicit ideas of what constitutes equitable distributions. They do this to have the flexibility to redress any concerns at their discretion. They do not use this policy as a way of engaging their stakeholders with the difficult conversations that often are part of equity discussions, nor do they use it to help further a common understanding of equity.

The Thomas Proctor High School is a good example of how controlled student choice can occur. Proctor is the lone high school in Utica, New York, which has a school-age population of 9,200 students, 70 percent receiving free or reduced-price lunch, 56 percent white, 26 percent black, and 12 percent Hispanic. Through a partnership with the local community college, Proctor was developing four career-based academies building on preexisting programs. Then the school caught the small school bug. It continued moving in the direction of career-based academies, and in 2004 opened as four separate small schools: science and technology; health, life, and environmental science; liberal arts; business and finance.

Proctor anticipated the potential student distribution problem that career-based themes could cause. To that end, it explicitly enacted a controlled choice policy, with an expectation that no demographic category would vary by more than plus or minus 10 percent from any school. Students were asked to list their top three choices. In general, based on first choices, enrollments fell within the range of the goal, with one main exception. The school for science and technology was overwhelmingly chosen by males, 283 to 37. As a consequence, two other schools were slightly overbalanced in terms of females, and the third slightly toward males. In looking at students' second preferences, the school was able to strike an equitable balance among all demographic factors. The end result? Seventy-five percent of students received their first choice. Only a handful of students switched schools during that first year.

Although, as in the Proctor example, assignment issues are frequently handled without continued difficulty, the school and the community should ideally be involved in and prepared for striking a balance between choice and equity. Students and parents will feel angst about school choices, and, depending on the types of schools offered, may feel that opportunities were lost. This issue is discussed at greater length in Chapter Six.

The Needs of Unique Populations

In one comprehensive high school, an administrator suggested placing all the special education students in one new small school, so that the school could best serve them. While this comment was made with good intentions, it signifies a lack of understanding of the established knowledge about the best methods to support special education students. As discussed in Chapter Six, it is possible to prepare all teachers to support special education students and English language learners; indeed, the instructional practices that support these students' learning also support the learning of regular education students. In this section, we touch upon issues of student choice of new schools.

We recommend that special education students be integrated to the fullest extent possible into each small school, along with their services and staffing. The method of special education delivery is decided upon by the individual autonomous small school, with heterogeneous grouping both the goal and the norm. As Shael Suransky of Bronx International High School notes, centralized support for these studies "goes to the heart of the instructional program of a school—how you deal with your kids who [need the most support academically]." Splitting these services undermines support for students and lessens the accountability for all adults to collectively ensure that their needs are met.

The situation for English language learners may differ. A technical assistance provider for ELL support noted that whether large or small, schools frequently lack trained teachers for these students. For example, a school may only have one Spanish bilingual certified algebra teacher. This leads to or adds to grouping or tracking and marginalization of ELL students and teachers in high schools. Clearly, unless a specific strategy is put in place in a conversion to address staff and resource needs, the resulting small schools are highly unlikely to have enough trained staff to support ELL students in each new school.

In one converting school that we observed, the numbers of ELL students appeared to be considerably underreported. Official numbers did not reflect the many students that needed language support—for instance, they excluded those students who were fluent in spoken English but had low levels of reading and writing fluency. In this comprehensive high school, as in many other such schools, ELL students gravitated to each other and to a few teachers who provided support. ELL teachers—themselves often marginalized in comprehensive schools and conversions—were marginalized on the design teams. A number reported that they either did not feel comfortable stepping forward to address ELL issues or felt silenced by colleagues in design team meetings. When the small schools opened, one school received more bilingual teachers than the others, while one administrator was assigned to oversee ELL students across all of the small schools in the shared facility. While the facility-wide administrator wanted to focus on support and instruction, the demands of assessment and testing took up most of her time.

Most conversions find that with their existing faculty they do not have enough trained staff to support language acquisition across multiple small schools. A result is often that trained staff are placed in a subset of small schools and ELL students may be asked to choose within that subset in order to receive appropriate support. School design, professional development, and faculty assignment will be a factor in how well the different new small autonomous schools serve students with special needs and English language learners. School choice policies will take this into account in trying to develop strategies that allow inclusion. As we discussed in Chapter Five, when we presented four school visions designed specifically with language acquisition needs in mind, the best way to support English language learners, given limited resources, may be to restrict their enrollment into fewer schools—while making sure that those schools are explicitly designed to best support their language acquisition needs.

Concluding Thoughts

Developing a school choice plan is a key decision point in creating and sustaining equitable schools. Children and families can now choose from a diverse portfolio of schools, each with a different focus, pedagogy, and philosophy. This move should create more quality options and greater equity in outcomes, yet it also has demonstrated the potential to increase long-standing inequity. Schools and districts should assess their choice plan and their plan to support special education students and English language learners with this in mind. We finish by noting the two key concerns of an equitable choice plan:

- How to best engage with parents who have been least engaged before to ensure that everyone has equal access to the information necessary to make informed choices for their children?

- How to create an equitable education in a district by providing choice and using fair assignment while preserving racial, ethnic, and class balance and integration?

Chapter 12

Teacher Assignment and Contractual Issues

THE MOVE from a comprehensive high school to a small school of the type we are striving to create necessitates a significant change in role for teachers. In traditional comprehensive high schools, teachers work mostly by themselves, teaching within one or two academic subject areas and gearing their instruction to whole classes of students. In the new small schools, teachers work collaboratively, frequently across disciplines. They seek to individualize instruction, and they usually wear several additional hats, often teaching multiple subjects, conducting advisory groups, and assuming leadership roles that break the confines of traditional teaching. Small schools draw on different sets of skills from each individual, and they rely on the synergy of teams of teachers working together. If everything works well, *all* of the new schools that emerge from a conversion have faculties with vision, skill, and enthusiasm about the new endeavor. But getting staff to this level requires some work.

This chapter explores key considerations in the staffing of small schools and in the reassignment of teachers from large comprehensive schools to new small ones. We explore how conversion processes can honor teachers' preferences regarding assignment while building powerful teaching teams at each school. We suggest a few core principles for thinking about the staffing process:

- Choice is crucial to teachers' sense of ownership and connection to the new school.

- Conversion is an opportunity to help teachers develop new professional skills.

- Each of the new autonomous schools needs to be staffed in a way that gives students access to quality teachers with the right background, knowledge, and skills for their small school.

Teaching in Small Schools

We need to acknowledge that many teachers are concerned that one by-product of the conversion process may be to eliminate teachers or teaching positions. To combat this, almost all the districts we have spoken with had the same maxim, "Everybody will have a job, but not the same job they had before." This reflects the desire to support staff, but also requires that staff be prepared to develop in new ways.

Schools and districts cannot invent this dream team of teachers. They need to work with the personnel they have, helping them grow and develop into the needed capacities. The conversion efforts we observed employed three strategies to help existing teachers grow professionally so small schools can craft staffs that consist of a committed, quality, and balanced professional team of teachers: professional development, development of interests, and leadership development. Helping teachers develop the skills they need to teach effectively in a small school also helps them develop the will to support the transformation rather than simply endure it.

Professional Development

Professional growth is a necessary and important part of the conversion process. In Chapter Six, we discuss some professional development needs that many conversions share. In preparing for their school's transformation, administrators should discuss with teachers their strengths, needs, and challenges, in the context of the curricular needs of the new schools. These conversations will help teachers determine the areas where they can build expertise to increase their effectiveness in the new schools.

By starting this process early, conversion planners give teachers more time to evaluate their needs and develop their skills. It is important for school districts to show that they are committed to working with teachers before teachers will willingly invest the time, effort, and often money required to take part in the effort wholeheartedly. For example, a chemistry teacher may need to develop an expertise in biology or physics to become more marketable and appealing to small schools. While such professional development is necessary, it is important to note that it is very challenging. Teachers who begin new degree programs can be supported by the district through waivers or other methods as they work to develop appropriate credentials. However, districts are under no obligation to pay for such degree programs.

Expand an Interest or Area of Expertise

Teachers have interests and expertise beyond their credentials. The creation of multiple autonomous small schools is an avenue for teachers' outside interests to be brought into their professional life. For example, Michelle Kennedy, teacher-leader of the Math, Science, and Technology Academy (MAST) in the West Clermont, Ohio, school district, says that at the beginning of their teacher assignment process, all the math and science teachers wanted to be part of their school because of its focus on math and science. Of course, not everyone could, because some of these same teachers had to be part of the other new schools. Through conversations, several of these teachers realized that they were drawn to the focus of other schools.

One math teacher with an interest in different cultures went to the School for World Studies. Another loved to sew and opted for the School of Creative Arts and Design. As Kennedy says:

> *Every child that comes into high school must take math. But when you teach math in the Creative Arts & Design High School you do so through art. For example, students might develop an understanding of geometric concepts through quilting with congruent triangles. In MAST we build bridges, we design our own experiments. When I ask my MAST kids to be artistic they get anxious. That's not how they learn and that's not why they chose this school.*

Leadership Positions

Small schools, as we have discussed, rely on distributed leadership. This provides multiple opportunities for leadership roles to be created for teachers, and such roles provide avenues for professional growth. In Indianapolis, the district plans on establishing a teaching and learning facilitator position to serve as an instructional coach and take on instructional leadership responsibilities. Each small school will also have an academic dean to handle the more typical administrative leadership role. The West Clermont district created the role of the small school coordinator, who teaches half time and serves as school coordinator the other half. They also have a project called Senior Exit Action, an advisory program, and other committees that distribute instructional leadership to teachers.

Contractual Concerns

We see the whole process of school conversion, and particularly the teacher assignment process, as an opportunity to expand expectations about the purposes and possibilities of schooling, to reenergize, and to draw on the unique strengths of all teachers. Charlotte Ciancio, superintendent of Mapleton Public Schools, believes that this process starts by creating, as a community, a strategic plan with a vision for schools based on students' needs. Further, knowing what roles, courses, and credentials are typical in small schools provides some guidelines for thinking about how the skills, talents, and certifications of a staff fit into the requirements of a small school. Ciancio says:

> *This last negotiation season we added new language to our contract around how this is going to work. . . . We agreed to a process that we would inform [teachers] at the beginning of the year that they have the year to either become highly qualified to work in one of the other environments or that they would begin their transition process so that they're leaving the system. We just want to make sure that they match whatever small school environment they may end up in. . . . We have had teachers who have chosen to leave the system because they want to work in comprehensive environments. We've tried to value that and tell people that sometimes the choices that we offer within a system require that you exit the system because your choice needs to be something different and we value that and appreciate that. You can't respect choice and only respect your own choice.*

Ciancio describes a philosophy in which the district plans ahead for its needs and works with its staff to help them develop the skills required to meet the needs of students most effectively. The district determines the necessary credentials for its teaching force and establishes options, such as temporary or emergency waivers, to help staff while they are getting appropriate credentials. Of course, this process of thinking about staffing and the needs of the school is not unique to conversions. It makes sense for all principals to sit down with staff each year to discuss the direction of the school, the ways in which teachers can contribute, and teachers' own professional goals. Teachers who expand their skills and their credentials are extremely valuable in any school system.

Teacher as Generalist

A challenge for small schools is that, at the high school level, many regulations support specialization. Small schools require their teachers to be generalists and to take on broader teaching responsibilities. For example, some small schools prefer their instruction to be integrated and interdisciplinary, requiring that teachers be adept in multiple academic traditions. Small school teachers are responsible for teaching electives based on their own nonacademic interests. The No Child Left Behind Act (NCLB) requires that teachers of core academic subjects be "highly qualified" in their content area. This has presented challenges for small schools and has made teachers with multiple credentials particularly strong candidates to work in small schools.

Warner-King and Price (2004) identified five ways that teachers in Washington State who have bachelor's degrees and teaching certificates can meet the NCLB "highly qualified" requirement. Although Warner-King and Price specifically examined one state, conversion efforts in other states may be able to take advantage of similar flexibilities in their own state laws and regulations:

- Explore Endorsement-Related Assignment Provisions
  Experienced teachers can demonstrate competency by teaching in an endorsement-related assignment area—that is, a group of courses that the local school board determines to include substantially the same subject matter as the endorsement.

- Petition for Out-of-Endorsement Assignment Waivers
  Experienced teachers can also meet the highly qualified definition with an out-of-endorsement assignment waiver. Small schools can petition local school districts or the State Board of Education to grant a waiver for an individual teacher, provided that the teacher has completed provisional status with the school district.

- HOUSSE Evaluation
  The HOUSSE provisions provide considerable flexibility for schools seeking to help experienced teachers demonstrate competency in a core academic subject. In Washington, the "high, objective, uniform state standard of evaluation" requires a satisfactory annual evaluation in the core academic subject based on the following criteria: instructional skill, classroom management, professional preparation and scholarship, effort toward improvement when needed, handling of student discipline and student problems, interest in teaching pupils, and knowledge of subject matter. Put simply, the HOUSSE provision allows teachers to demonstrate competency through an annual evaluation by a certified administrator, such as a principal. While some observers contend that the use of the annual evaluation essentially gives a school carte blanche to declare any existing teacher highly qualified, the state superintendent's office responds that it has confidence in the professionalism of certified administrators. The law outlines the legal requirements for annual evaluations; violations of these requirements can result in unprofessional conduct charges and possible revocation of the administrator's certification.

- Use Conditional and Emergency Certification Procedures
  In Washington, teachers with conditional or emergency certificates meet the highly qualified requirement, as long as they are enrolled in a residency teacher preparation program (including alternative routes programs). They are also required to complete the program and earn a residency certificate within one year for emergency certificate holders, and within three years for conditional certificate holders.

- Implement Parent Communication Requirements Around Highly Qualified Teachers

If a teacher in a school receiving Title I funds does not meet the definition of highly qualified for a particular content area, he or she is allowed to teach in that area as long as the school notifies parents. Small schools can use the parental notification as an opportunity to inform parents about the teacher's overall experience and the characteristics that make the teacher highly effective, if not highly qualified under the law. The Office of the Superintendent of Public Instruction has posted sample letters on its website that schools may use in fulfilling their notification requirements [Warner-King & Price, 2004, pp. 38–40].

In addition, Warner-King and Price note two other ways that small schools can support generalist teachers within these legal requirements:

- *Team teaching:* Teachers award credit within their content area.
- *Dual certification:* Where, for example, humanities teachers hold endorsements in both English and social studies.

Seniority Rights

One reason that small schools have been successful is that they are staffed by a committed group of like-minded educators, who typically go through extensive professional development together (Raywid & Schmerler, 2003). This often runs counter to a long-standing teachers' union provision: the right to fill openings based on seniority within the system. A small school's effectiveness is undermined if a teacher new to the school does not agree with the school's pedagogical and philosophical approach. Some unions, such as New York City's United Federation of Teachers, endorse an arrangement that suspends seniority transfer rights if a certain percentage of teachers within a school agree. The school staff selects new hires. In schools with staff who have not bought in to the school vision, it is vital that committed staff have created a healthy professional culture that can integrate such staff or survive the lack of buy-in. One costly but often workable solution to this problem is to hire teachers as permanent substitutes if they are not chosen by any school.

Counseling Teachers Out

Some administrators make a point of acknowledging to their staff that wanting to be a teacher in a large school is a valid choice. In multi-school districts, where not every school is converting, the district can create a process for such teachers to remain in the district. In a small district, or one in which every school is converting, this is not an option. In these situations, it is especially important to have a conversation about teacher and district needs at the beginning of the conversion process (and to continue such conversations each year as good practice) and to provide support for finding jobs in other districts for the teachers who might wish to continue teaching in a large comprehensive high school.

Teacher Assignment Strategies, Policies, Procedures

Because their communities are so small, each teacher in a small school has the potential of having a relatively big impact on the culture of the school. A powerful staff at a small autonomous school would

- Be balanced in disciplines and curricular coverage
- Believe in the instructional style and mission of the school
- Be a cohesive group (have the communication and conflict resolution skills to be able to work together)
- Reflect demographic balance
- Reflect a range of experiences

In this section, we describe strategies that have been used to assign teachers to new autonomous small schools. There are, of course, trade-offs to decisions regarding teacher assignment. We outline six teacher assignment strategies and then explore the strengths and challenges inherent in each. We also acknowledge that often these procedures are not independent of each other; they can be used in combination. District, school, and union staff all have a say in creating these policies.

- Using a controlled choice process
- Building from teacher team and small learning communities
- Using small school design team as a core of teachers at the school
- Applying random assignment
- Invoking the district's current policies
- Developing a volunteer plan if the roll-out will be staged across several school years

Using a Controlled Choice Process

In this assignment procedure, teachers list their preferences for schools, and are divided based on their preferences and discipline, experience, sex, race, or other relevant factors. In this way, teachers' interest is a part of the process, but the district can meet the need for each school to have a balanced group of teachers.

Building from Small Learning Communities

Some large high schools undergoing conversion have small learning community (SLC) structures already in place or have developed such communities before they move to autonomous small schools. A natural choice for teacher assignment is to go with their SLC—if it's working. How do you analyze current success levels? Consider the following questions:

- Is the SLC serving all students effectively?
- Does it have a compelling philosophy of learning?
- Do staff have the type of collaborative relationships that support a small school?
- Does it have a vision in keeping with the larger aims of the conversion?

Using Design Team Members as the Core of New Faculty

In some cases, a small school design team with a core of teachers has formed, typically through an open RFP process or some other voluntary method in which teachers of a school can choose whether or not to be members of a design team. Again, this appears to be a natural group to form the core of a new autonomous small school's staff. Who better to have on board than the people who designed the school?

In some districts, however, professional staff members on the design team are not guaranteed a place on that school's faculty. All the hiring is done according to the district's regular policy for staffing schools. In one such district, though, the union agreed that even though the rules weren't in place to guarantee this assignment, staffing with the design team was in the best interest of the teachers and the new schools, and so created a policy to support it.

Applying Random Assignment

In Chapter Five, we described how some districts are creating multiple small schools without formed identities. The expectation is that staff and students will create that identity together over time. In these situations, it makes sense for a district to randomly (or mostly randomly) divide staff into small schools based on discipline, experience, sex, race, or other factors. However, in situations where schools already have an identity in place, this process will most likely assign staff to schools where there is not a best fit.

Invoking the District's Current Policies

Districts with multiple high schools already have a teacher assignment policy in place, although this policy may or may not best fit the needs for the conversion of large schools. For example, some conversion districts have been limited in their teacher assignment policy by a "building rights" rule. In this rule, teachers with seniority have the right to remain in the building of their choice. However, this limits each small school's ability to organize a group of like-minded teachers. Like any other district policy that currently exists and relates to a conversion task, it is important to reconceptualize that policy with a view to the guiding vision of what the new educational system will be.

Developing a Volunteer Plan

If a conversion school phases in the creation of new autonomous schools, either by grade or by school, then some teachers will remain in the large school while others go to the new small schools. In these situations, new schools get the faculty who want to work in each small school or are most committed to the new small schools. This can work well, but the conversion team needs to be aware of the danger of overstocking one or two of the early schools with the most experienced or enthusiastic teachers.

Integrating New Staff into a Developing Culture

An issue that arises when building from small learning communities, or when phasing in grades over time, is how to add new staff to a core group of teachers. This is particularly challenging if the small school does not have autonomy in choosing and hiring its own staff. One principal described the problem in these terms:

> You went from a group of people that voluntarily participated in small teams to everybody being assigned to a school that didn't necessarily agree with [their own philosophy] and going to teams of twenty. That was frustrating for those that didn't totally agree with it and for those that did because now they had to work with each other. And there hadn't been ever really any foundation laid for that team dynamic to play out.

It is possible to minimize teacher assignment and ownership issues during the design phase by keeping all staff informed about the work of the design teams throughout the process, and by encouraging as many staff as possible to join with or participate in meaningful ways with the new school designs. This can be done formally, through reports during staff meetings, or informally, making sure that a design team touches base with other teachers about current plans.

Just as small schools need a culture of high expectations for students, they also need one for staff. One of the goals in creating schools is to help them to develop a healthy professional culture. In such a culture, teachers display ownership of their school, are committed to meeting the needs of the students they serve, and are the keepers of the vision of their school. They also are responsible for recruiting, hiring (if allowed), and integrating new members into their professional community. In recruiting and hiring new staff, a school clearly sets expectations. Having students and parents on hiring committees sets one tone; requiring applicants to teach lessons sets expectations about the level of collaboration that the school expects.

Other Teacher Assignment Challenges

We have already discussed the assignment strategies for special education and English language learner teachers in Chapter Eleven. Specialist teachers are another group that also has unique assignment challenges.

The Role of Specialist Teachers

An important difference between small and large schools is in their curricular offerings. Large comprehensive schools offer a smorgasbord curriculum that attempts to meet student interests by adding new classes. Small schools meet the needs of student interest by personalizing within classes. When thinking about teacher assignment, this leads to some challenges for teachers in specialist positions, such as health, physical education, home economics, and art.

Specialist teachers have two options: either the new schools need skills very similar to what they have, or the schools need them to develop new skills. Some schools hire physical education teachers from other schools to work part-time. Other schools build physical education into the whole program. As an example of the latter approach, the Wellness Program at Quest High School (in Humble, Texas) is fully integrated into school life. It far surpasses the state requirements for physical education and has a health as well as a physical education component. Wellness is intended to help students develop the skills for a physically active lifestyle through exploring different activities, developing different mental and physical skill sets, and learning how to integrate wellness activities into their day. The health education component culminates with a written project that reflects on their previous years and projects their hopes for a healthy lifestyle in the future.

Students fulfill a forty-hour/semester requirement, divided equally among strength and stretching, cardiovascular activity, skill development, and social activities. This ensures that students take part in a wide variety of activities, from yoga or weight training to walking or running, dodge ball or football—or Ping Pong. According to Holly Schoettlin, the wellness coordinator, students design their own personal wellness plan based on a fitness test they take at the beginning of each semester and monitor and reassess their progress.

Only ninth-grade students have a wellness period; all other students incorporate their physical education activities into their school day. Students do so during independent study periods, the school's advisory program (in which classes can engage in intramural sports), a monthly after-school wellness field trip (bowling, rock climbing, roller skating), and in academic classes. When the school organized a Space Day as part of the space curriculum, for example, wellness was one activity. Students participated in activities similar to those of astronaut training—balance, reaction time—and had their scores compared to those of astronauts. During some students' service learning science project, participants receive cardiovascular credit for the two-to-four-mile hike they take to collect water samples.

Of course, many specialized teachers and their programs have been under the gun for some time and have made modifications to their practice. One home economics teacher who was worried about the phase-out of her job worked to integrate more focused academic content into her course and created interdisciplinary courses with science and technology teachers. By focusing on the scientific aspects of nutrition and by using technology to support her instructional practice, this teacher stretched herself in significant ways, provided a high-quality education to her students, and created a powerful niche for herself.

Concluding Thoughts

We offer the following four final thoughts:

- Districts have to think ahead: contracts must communicate the kind of expectations that districts have for teachers. Districts also need to offer support for teachers to meet these expectations.

- Small school creation provides opportunities for powerful professional development.

- It is very hard for people to change, especially in mid-career. The change will not be perfect at first and should be thought of as a transition, a work in process.

- The most important thing is that teachers be committed to the kind of new small school that they are part of. Credentials and capacity building can (or at least should) follow commitment.

Chapter 13
Concluding Thoughts

FORMING NEW small automonous schools is one step in the transformation of educational practice. It is one step toward providing all young people with an intellectually engaging, personalized, and equitable education that will prepare them for success in today's society. Moving from large to small creates conditions that facilitate the success of all students—and of the adults who work with them.

But the transformation of existing high schools to small schools is just one step. As we described in Chapter One, conversion requires much more than changing school size. It means a paradigm shift for everyone—students, teachers, and community members—to a new definition of what schools do and what they look like, and what students need to know and how they really learn—and how they should be taught. Conversion is qualitatively different from reform; it seeks to transform our school system, not fix it.

We are learning more about reinvention every day. Those involved in conversion are constantly looking to those one step ahead to see what they might learn. The creation of new autonomous small schools has never been tried on this scale before. We can expect difficulties, even some failures. But the research on effective small schools is clear: they can educate all students well. Taking small schools to scale to create a system where all students can succeed is a worthy and achievable goal. It is achievable if the educational community—those working inside schools and those who support them—learns from the successes and missteps of those who came before. It is achievable if we do not let the challenges of the work keep our communities from the goal of having all students succeed. We offer three themes to take away . . .

Create a Vision with Students at the Center

As Sarason (1991) writes, schools exist exclusively for students. This is why many change efforts have begun by envisioning what their ideal graduate would look like, by thinking about what students need to know and be able to do and what forms of evidence are required to demonstrate mastery of skills and subjects. Others begin by thinking about their own best learning experience, sharing these powerful experiences with their teams, and designing their pedagogy, school structure, and culture based on their commonalities. The important idea is to engage people in visualizing what successful students and education looks like, because looking at one's practice in the context of the student outcomes one seeks drives the development of effective school design, practice, and culture.

We all know that initiating and sustaining change is difficult in schools. Holding a vision of what learning looks like, of the relationships and daily life of a vibrant school, is vital to keeping a change effort focused on what it takes to educate every student to be college ready, to be productive in an information society, and to be an active and reflective citizen in a diverse society. Putting students at the center keeps the effort moving successfully forward.

Be Transformative

Those familiar with schools are used to waves of reform: there's a problem, let's put money into it; let's create a program to fix it; the reform is a Band-Aid and meets institutional resistance. It doesn't work, people blame the reform, it's over and they find something new. Decades of cycles of reform underscore the bedrock truth that reform does not work; what we need is *reinvention*. To meet our goal of educating every student requires keeping our eyes firmly on this vision of reinvention, of changing the structures, the relationships, and the policies to support this goal. Effective conversion leaders are aware they are challenging the prevailing cultural image and institutional reality of the high school. They build in time and space for crafting a new vision of schools and districts with their students, teachers, and community members. Remaking school structures, designs, pedagogy, and culture—transformation—requires the commitment of a large group of stakeholders—students, parents, community members, and educators.

Nurture and Support the New Schools

Conversion is a step toward a goal—the goal of creating a comprehensive system of schools in which districts have a portfolio of high-quality schools with different philosophies, pedagogies, and cultures that provide options for students and families. Students today need to be prepared for an Information Age society. They need the skills to be lifelong learners, analytical thinkers, effective communicators, and engaged members of an active democracy. Small autonomous schools have the flexibility to create and take advantage of those conditions we know lead to sustained student learning.

Once small schools are formed, it's just the beginning. Conversion, for all its effort and all its challenges, is only a part of the hard work of reinvention. It is one of a number of important and hard steps. While we believe that much of what occurs during the conversion process can prepare educators and community members for the types of relationships they will have and the skills they need to be successful in small schools, there will be growing pains. Once new small autonomous schools are formed, the community must focus on ensuring their success and sustainability. It must support their development into an effective community of learners. Educators need policies that support small school autonomy and flexibility, time to collaborate to take advantage of their more personalized relationships, and ongoing training and support in the new instructional styles they may be using. Most of all, they need the capacity to engage in cycles of inquiry that ensure the vision and missions are being carried out and practice constantly refined.

If converting from large comprehensive schools to small schools is a powerful step toward reinvention in the moment, we can count on the fact that the new schools will continue to need to reinvent themselves over time. Indeed, it is one of the strengths of smallness that it makes ongoing reinvention more viable. As we proceed together to create powerful schools for all our children, we can take heart in setting a precedent of the possibility of reinvention on a truly historic scale.

Appendix A
Profiled Organizations

The following are sources of information on the small autonomous school movement.

The Bay Area Coalition for Equitable Schools
1720 Broadway, Fourth Floor
Oakland, CA 94612-2106
Voice: (510) 208-0160
Web: www.bayces.org

Big Picture Company
17 Gordon Avenue, Suite 104
Providence, RI 02905
Voice: (401) 781-1873
Web: www.bigpicture.org

Bill & Melinda Gates Foundation
P.O. Box 23350
Seattle, WA 98102
Voice: (206) 709-3140
Web: www.gatesfoundation.org

California Tomorrow
1904 Franklin Street, Suite 300
Oakland, CA 94612
Voice: (510) 496-0220
Web: www.californiatomorrow.org

Center for Applied Special Technology (CAST)
40 Harvard Mills Square, Suite 3
Wakefield, MA 01880-3233
Voice: (781) 245-2212
Web: www.cast.org

The Center for Collaborative Education
1 Renaissance Park
1135 Tremont Street, Suite 490
Boston, MA 02120
Voice: (617) 421-0134
Web: www.ccebos.org

CES Northwest
School of Education
University of Puget Sound
Tacoma, WA 98416
Voice: (253) 879-3807
Web: www.cesnorthwest.org

The Civil Rights Project
125 Mt. Auburn Street,
3rd Floor
Cambridge, MA 02138
Voice: (617) 496-6367
Web: www.civilrightsproject.harvard.edu

Coalition of Essential Schools
1814 Franklin Street,
Suite 700
Oakland, CA 94612
Voice: (510) 433-1451
Web: www.essentialschools.org

The Education Alliance
222 Richmond Street, Suite 300
Providence, RI 02903
Voice: (800) 521-9550 or (401) 274-9548
Web: www.lab.brown.edu

Education Resource Strategies
8 Bennett Road
Wayland, MA 01778
Voice: (508) 276-1161
Web: educationresourcestrategies.org

Expeditionary Learning
100 Mystery Point Road
Garrison, NY 10524
Voice: (845) 424-4000
Web: www.elob.org

FairTest
342 Broadway
Cambridge, MA 02139-1802
Voice: (617) 864-4810
Web: www.fairtest.org

Greater Cleveland Regional Transit Authority (GCRTA)
1240 West 6th Street
Cleveland, OH 44113-1331
Voice: (216) 566-5100
Web: www.gcrta.org

Harwood Institute for Public Innovation
4915 St. Elmo Avenue, Suite 402
Bethesda, MD 20814
Voice: (301) 656-3669
Web: www.theharwoodinstitute.org

Jobs for the Future
88 Broad Street
Boston, MA 02110
Voice: (617) 728-4446
Web: www.jff.org

KnowledgeWorks Foundation
1 West 4th Street, Suite 200
Cincinnati, OH 45202
Voice: (513) 929-4777
Web: www.kwfdn.org

Leading for Equity, Achievement, and Democracy (LEAD)
1720 Broadway, Fourth Floor
Oakland, CA 94612-2106
Voice: (510) 208-0160
Web: www.bayces.org/programs_services/lead/

National Association of Secondary School Principals
1904 Association Drive
Reston, VA 20191-1537
Voice: (703) 860-0200
Web: www.nassp.org

National School Reform Faculty
Harmony Education Center
P.O. Box 1787
Bloomington, IN 47402
Voice: (812) 330-2702
Web: www.nsrfharmony.org

Oakland Community Organizations
7200 Bancroft Avenue
#2 Eastmont Mall (upper level)
Oakland, CA 94605
Voice: (510) 639-1444
Web: www.oaklandcommunity.org

The Principal Residency Network
1 Renaissance Park
1135 Tremont Street, Suite 490
Boston, MA 02120
Voice: (617) 421-0134
Web: www.ccebos.org/gbprn

The Regional Teachers Center at Francis W. Parker Charter Essential School
49 Antietam Street
Devens, MA 01434
Voice: (978) 772-2687
Web: www.parker.org/rtc

School Redesign Network
Stanford University
School of Education
520 Galvez Mall
Stanford, CA 94305-3084
Voice: (650) 725-0703
Web: www.schoolredesign.net

Small Schools Project
7900 East Greenlake Drive North, Suite 212
Seattle, WA 98103
Voice: (206) 812-3160
Web: www.smallschoolsproject.org

Small Schools Workshop
1608 North Milwaukee Avenue, Suite 912
Chicago, IL 60647
(773) 384-1030
Web: www.smallschoolsworkshop.org

Profiled Schools

Boston Arts Academy
Shares building with Fenway High School
174 Ipswich Street
Boston, MA 02215
Web: www.boston-arts-academy.org

Bronx High School for the Visual Arts
New small school located in a building of its own (previously located on
the Columbus High School campus)
2040 Antin Place
Bronx, NY 10462

Bronx International High School
New small school located in Morris High School campus
1110 Boston Road
Bronx, NY 10456

Brookhaven High School
Large high school becoming multiple small schools
4077 Karl Road
Columbus, OH 43224

Clover Park High School
Large high school becoming multiple small schools
11023 Gravelly Lake Drive SW
Lakewood, WA 98499-1391
Web: http://cpsd.cloverpark.k12.wa.us/Schools/HighSchools/CPHS/
CloverPark.asp

Columbus High School
Large high school sharing building with multiple small schools
925 Astor Avenue
Bronx, NY 10469

Entrepreneurship High School
Newly created school located in converted South Shore High School campus
7529 South Constance Avenue
Chicago, IL 60624

Federal Hocking High School
Freestanding small autonomous school
8461 State Route 144
Stewart, OH 45778
Web: www.federalhocking.k12.oh.us

Fenway High School
Shares building with Boston Arts Academy
174 Ipswich Street
Boston, MA 02215
Web: http://fenway.boston.k12.ma.us

Foster High School
Large high school becoming multiple small schools
4242 S. 144th Street
Tukwila, WA 98168

Global Enterprise Academy
New small school located in Columbus High School campus
925 Astor Avenue
Bronx, NY 10469

International High School
New small school located on LaGuardia Community College campus
31–10 Thomson Avenue
Long Island City, NY 11101

Julia Richman Complex
Includes six small schools on its campus:
- Urban Academy
- Vanguard High School
- Talent Unlimited High School
- P226M Junior High Annex
- The Ella Baker School

- Manhattan International High School
  317 East 67th Street
  New York, NY 10021
  Web: www.jrec.org

LaGuardia Middle College High School
Public school serving grades 9–12 and the first two years of college
LaGuardia Community College
31–10 Thompson Avenue
Long Island City, NY 11101

Leominster High School
Large high school becoming multiple small schools
122 Granite Street
Leominster, MA 01453

Life Academy
Hothoused from large high school and now freestanding
2111 International Boulevard
Oakland, CA 94601

Marble Hill School for International Studies
New small school located in John F. Kennedy High School campus
99 Terrace View Avenue
Bronx, NY 10463
http://marblehill.newvisionsk12.org

The Metropolitan Regional Career and Technical Center (The Met)
Small autonomous school
Public Street Campus
325 Public Street
Providence, RI 02905
Web: www.metcenter.org

Pablo Neruda Academy for Architecture and World Studies
New small school located in the Adlai Stevenson High School campus
1980 Lafayette Avenue
Bronx, NY 10473

Pelham Preparatory Academy
New small school located in Columbus High School campus
925 Astor Avenue
Bronx, NY 10469

Quest High School
Small autonomous school, shares campus with community organizations
18901 Timber Forest Drive
Humble, TX 77346
Web: http://qhs.humble.k12.tx.us/

School of Environmental Studies
12155 Johhny Cake Ridge Road
Apple Valley, MN 55124

School of the Arts High School in Chicago
New small school located in converted South Shore High School campus
7529 South Constance Avenue
Chicago, IL 60624

Shaw High School
Large high school becoming multiple small schools
15320 Euclid Avenue
East Cleveland, OH 44112

Skyview High School
Large high school becoming multiple small schools
9000 York Street
Thornton, CO 80229

Thomas Proctor High School
Large high school becoming multiple small schools
1203 Hilton Avenue
Utica, NY 13501

Tyeew High School
Large high school becoming multiple small schools
4424 S. 188th Street
SeaTac, WA 98188

West Clermont School District
Glen Este Campus
4342 Glen Este-Withamsville Road
Cincinnati, OH 45245-1599
- School for American Studies
- School for Scientific Studies
- School of Applied Health Sciences
- WeCIPA

- School of Communications and Technology
  Amelia Campus
  1351 Clough Pike
  Batavia, OH 45103-2546
- School of Creative Arts and Design
- International Baccalaureate School
- Math, Science and Technology Academy
- School for World Studies
- Business and Technology School

Youth Empowerment School
Now freestanding, first year was located in the converted Fremont High
School campus
4610 Foothill Boulevard
Oakland, CA 94601

Appendix C
Additional School Design Resources

General

References

Ancess, J. (2003). *Beating the odds: High schools as communities of commitment.* New York: Teachers College Press.

Clinchy, E. (Ed.). (2000). *Creating new schools: How small schools are changing American education.* New York: Teachers College Press.

Darling-Hammond, L. (2001). *The right to learn: A blueprint for creating schools that work.* San Francisco: Jossey-Bass.

Meier, D. (1995). *The power of their ideas: Lessons for America from a small school in Harlem.* Boston: Beacon Press.

Meier, D. (2002). *In schools we trust: Creating communities of learning in an era of testing and standardization.* Boston: Beacon Press.

Sizer, T. R. (1984). *Horace's compromise: The dilemma of the American high school.* Boston: Houghton Mifflin.

Sizer, T. R. (1992). *Horace's school: Redesigning the American high school.* Boston: Houghton Mifflin.

Sizer, T. R. (1996). *Horace's hope: What works for the American high school.* Boston: Houghton Mifflin.

Toch, T. (2003). *High schools on a human scale: How small schools can transform American education.* Boston: Beacon Press.

Wood, G. (1993). *Schools that work: America's most innovative public education programs.* New York: Plume.

Teaching and Learning

General Topics

Zimmermann, S., & Keene, E. (1997). *Mosaic of thought: Teaching comprehension in a reader's workshop.* Portsmouth, NH: Heinemann.

Cousins, E., Mednick, A., & Campbell, M. (Eds.). (2000). *Literacy all day long.* Dubuque, IA: Kendall Hunt.

Authentic Achievement

Newmann, F., & Associates. (1996). *Authentic achievement: Restructuring schools for intellectual quality.* San Francisco: Jossey-Bass.

Differentiated Instruction

Tomlinson, C. A. (2001). *How to differentiate instruction in mixed-ability classrooms* (2nd Ed.). Alexandria, VA: Association for Supervision and Curriculum Development.

Tomlinson, C. A., & Allan, S. D. (2000). *Leadership for differentiating schools and classrooms.* Alexandria, VA: Association for Supervision and Curriculum Development.

Curriculum

Reference

Steinberg, A., Cushman, K., & Riordan, R. (1999). *Schooling for the real world.* San Francisco: Jossey-Bass.

Organizations

Facing History and Ourselves
National Office
16 Hurd Road
Brookline, MA 02445
Voice: (617) 232-1595
Fax: (617) 232-0281
Web: www.facinghistory.org/

The Algebra Project, Inc.
99 Bishop Allen Drive
Cambridge, MA 02139
Voice: (617) 491-0200
Web: www.algebra.org

The Buck Institute for Education

18 Commercial Boulevard
Novato, CA 94949
Voice: (415) 883-0122
Fax: (415) 883-0260
E-mail: info@bie.org
Web: www.bie.org

The Buck Institute for Education (BIE) is a research and development organization working to make schools and classrooms more effective through the use of problem- and project-based instruction. BIE outlines five components necessary for project work—content, driving questions, components, strategies, and assessment.

Performance Assessments

Reference

Wiggins, G., & McTighe, J. (1998). *Understanding by design.* Alexandria, VA: Association for Supervision and Curriculum Development.

Organizations

New York Performance Standards Consortium

Web: www.performanceassessment.org

The New York Performance Standards Consortium represents twenty-eight schools across New York State. Formed in 1997, the Consortium opposes high-stakes tests, arguing that one size does not fit all. The New York Performance Standards Consortium has developed an assessment system that leads to quality teaching that enhances rather than compromises our students' education.

Fairtest: National Center for Fair and Open Testing

342 Broadway
Cambridge, MA 02139-1802
E-mail: fairtest@fairtest.org
Voice: (617) 864-4810
Web: www.fairtest.org

What Kids Can Do

P.O. Box 603252
Providence, RI 02906
Voice: (401) 247-7665
E-mail: info@whatkidscando.org
Web: www.whatkidscando.org

What Kids Can Do reminds us that demonstrations of what students know and can do occupies the heart of education and all attempts to evaluate its outcomes. What Kids Can Do makes the connection between student accomplishments, school-evaluated academic achievement, and critical life skills, and makes us unable to forget that learning is complex, endlessly unique, and deeply personal.

Learning Record Online

E-mail: syverson@utscc.utexas.edu

Web: www.cwrl.utexas.edu/~syverson/olr

The Learning Record assessment model provides ways for schools to establish a performance-based authentic assessment system rich in data collection and analysis. Focusing on individualized assessments in K–12 reading and mathematics, it allows teachers opportunities to ensure interrater reliability across schools regionally. The Learning Record makes it possible for schools to develop a comprehensive system that deals rigorously with accountability questions while keeping the focus on personalized teaching and learning.

Equity

Organizations

CREDE—Center for Research on Education, Diversity & Excellence

University of California, Santa Cruz

1156 High Street

Santa Cruz, CA 95064

Voice: (831) 459-3500

Fax: (831) 459-3502

E-mail: crede@cats.ucsc.edu

Web: www.crede.org/standards/standards.html

The Five Standards for Effective Pedagogy are practices that have proven effective for all students, and have been especially successful with typically marginalized students. The five standards establish principles for best teaching and are an accessible and safe way to start discussions with teachers surrounding equity in their practice.

Southern Poverty Law Center

400 Washington Avenue

Montgomery, AL 36104

Voice: (334) 956-8200

Web: www.tolerance.org

A project of the Southern Poverty Law Center, Tolerance.org features extensive civil rights–related resources for teachers, parents, teens, and younger children. The Web site reflects the work of *Teaching Tolerance* magazine, and includes a wide range of anti-bias curricula, an online educators' discussion area, professional development material, and more.

The Civil Rights Project at Harvard University

125 Mt. Auburn Street, 3rd Floor
Cambridge, MA 02138
Voice: (617) 496-6367
Fax: (617) 495-5210
E-mail: crp@harvard.edu
Web: www.civilrightsproject.harvard.edu

The Civil Rights Project Web site focuses extensively on education-related issues, sponsoring conferences and other gatherings, amassing news items relevant to equity work in education, issuing civil rights alerts and studies. The site's resources section maps useful paths to related organizations' work.

English Language Learners

Organizations

California Tomorrow

1904 Franklin Street, Suite 300
Oakland, CA 94612
Voice: (510) 496-0220
Web: www.californiatomorrow.org

Center for Applied Linguistics (CAL)

4646 40th Street, NW
Washington, DC 20016-1859
Voice: (202) 362-0700
Fax: (202) 362-3740
E-mail: info@cal.org
Web: www.cal.org

CAL's mission is "to promote and improve the teaching and learning of languages, identify and solve problems related to language and culture, and serve as a resource for information about language and culture." Its Web site does that splendidly, featuring extensive information for English language teachers. CAL is a good first stop when you're researching ESL and bilingual teaching and learning topics; its links to databases, CAL-run services, and outside links offer a broad perspective and current panorama of just about anything you'd need to know.

Portraits of Success

c/o María Estela Brisk
Lynch School of Education
Boston College
140 Commonwealth Avenue
Chestnut Hill, MA 02467
Voice: (617) 552-4216
Fax: (617) 552-1840
E-mail: portraits@lab.brown.edu
Web: www.alliance.brown.edu/pubs/pos/

A joint project of the National Association for Bilingual Education, Boston College, and the Northeast and Islands Regional Educational Laboratory at Brown University, Portraits of Success presents detailed profiles of seven distinct schools that are examples of successful bilingual education. Each profile includes a description of the school's bilingual program, student outcomes, community response, program funding, and contact information. The Web site also contains a helpful annotated bibliography of research on effective bilingual practices.

Teaching Diverse Learners

Web: www.alliance.brown.edu/tdl/

A Web site dedicated to enhancing the capacity of teachers to work effectively and equitably with English language learners. It provides access to information—publications, educational materials, and the work of experts in the field—that promotes high achievement for these students.

Special Education

References

Fink, R. P. (1995/1996). Successful dyslexics: A constructivist study of passionate interest reading. *Journal of Adolescent and Adult Literacy, 39*(4), 268–278.

Ford, C., & Fitterman, L. J. (1994). *Collaborative consultation: Literature review and case study of a proposed alternative delivery system.* Education Resources Information Center, www.eric.ed.gov. (ED 374 633).

Garcia, S. B., & Ortiz, A. A. (1998). Preventing inappropriate referrals of language minority students to special education. *National Clearinghouse for Bilingual Education,* pp. 149–160.

Garnett, K. (1994). *Thinking about inclusion and learning disabilities: A teacher's guide.* Division for Learning Disabilities of the Council for Exceptional Children. Available online: www.ldonline.org/article.php?max=20&id=502&loc=26. Access date: May 2, 2005.

Orbitz, A. (2001). *English language learners with special needs: Effective instructional strategies.* ERIC Clearinghouse on Languages and Linguistics. (ED 469 207). Available online: www.ldonline.org/ld2/test/article.php?max=20&id=744&loc=51. Access date: May 2, 2005.

Pavri, S. (2000, Fall). The social face of inclusive education: Are students with learning disabilities really included in the classroom. *Preventing School Failure.* Available online: www.ldonline.org/article.php?max=20&id=500&loc=51. Access date: May 2, 2005.

Quenneville, J. (2001). Tech tools for students with learning disabilities: Infusion into inclusive classrooms. *Preventing School Failure, 45*(4), 167–170. Available online: www.ldonline.org/article.php?max=20&special_grouping=&id=456&loc=72. Access date: May 2, 2005.

Tomlinson, C. A., & Allan, S. D. (2000). Communicating with parents and the public about differentiation. In *Leadership for Differentiating Schools and Classrooms.* Alexandria, VA: Association for Supervision and Curriculum Development.

Tomlinson, C. A., & Allan, S. D. (2000). Staff development that supports differentiation. In *Leadership for Differentiating Schools and Classrooms.* Alexandria, VA: Association for Supervision and Curriculum Development.

Zabala, J. S. (1998). *Get SETT for successful inclusion and transition.* Available online: www.ldonline.org/article.php?max=20&id=504&loc=27. Access date: May 2, 2005.

Organizations

LD Online

Web: www.ldonline.org

LD Online provides resources for people with disabilities and their parents, educators, and friends. Its comprehensive offerings include descriptions of a wide range of learning disabilities, expert commentary, pointers to school, summer, and other programs, an active online community, research collections with active links to full articles from a variety of sources, and more.

Continuous Improvement Process
Reference

Bernhardt, V. (1994). *The school portfolio.* Princeton Junction, NJ: Eye on Education.

Organizations

Education for the Future

400 West First Street

Chico, CA 95929-0230

Voice: (530) 898-4482

Fax: (530) 898-4484

E-mail: effinfo@csuchico.edu

Web: http://eff.csuchico.edu/home/

Education for the Future, directed by Victoria Bernhardt, is a nonprofit initiative located on the campus of California State University, Chico. It focuses on working with schools, districts, state departments of education, and other educational service centers and agencies on systemic change and comprehensive data analyses that lead to increased student learning.

Personalization and Advisories

Reference

Poliner, R., & Lieber, C. M. (2004). *The advisory guide: Designing and implementing effective advisory programs in secondary schools.* Cambridge, MA: Educators for Social Responsibility.

Organizations

Educators for Social Responsibility—National Center

23 Garden Street

Cambridge, MA 02138

Voice: (617) 492-1764

E-mail: educators@esrnational.org

Web: www.esrnational.org/resources.htm

The Wildwood Outreach Center

Web: www.wildwood.org/outreach/workshops.asp

Based at the Wildwood School in Los Angeles, the Wildwood Outreach Center provides workshops in which participants learn about the benefits that a structured advisory program can have in their school or get new ideas on how to improve an existing advisory program. The workshop includes information on advisory purpose and design, curriculum, protocols, implementation training and reference materials. Wildwood also offers The Advisory Toolkit, a step-by-step guide for educators who want to create or enhance an advisory program at their school. The Advisory Toolkit consists of a forty-five-minute DVD on the advisory programs at four schools, accompanied by a detailed workbook.

The Regional Teachers Center at Francis W. Parker Charter Essential School
49 Antietam Street
Devens, MA 01434
Voice: (978) 772-2687
Web: www.parker.org/rtc

The Regional Teachers Center, in Devens, Massachusetts, offers a range of professional development opportunities including a two-day institute focusing on advisory program design, giving participants an opportunity to create a vision for an advisory program and develop a plan for successful implementation. Participants will leave the institute with an understanding of the importance of developing consensus around a clearly defined purpose; materials and structures to help think about questions of program organization; examples of advisory content, including several commonly used protocols and routines; tools designed to assess program effectiveness; and samples of professional development plans to ensure the successful implementation and ongoing support for an advisory program.

New Visions
320 West 13th Street
New York, NY 10014

New Visions provides a fifteen-page document (available online at www.newvisions.org/schoolsuccess/downloads/StudentAdv.pdf) that is a succinct overview of high school advisory programs. Of particular note are descriptions of advisories at three New York City schools—Baruch College Campus High School, the Beacon School, and the New York City Museum School—that detail the programs' structure, curriculum, and adviser role.

Professional Learning Communities, Collaboration Practices, and Organizations
Reference
Sergiovanni, T. J. (1994). *Building community in schools.* San Francisco: Jossey-Bass.

Organizations
Looking at Student Work
Web: www.lasw.org

This Web site homes in on the effort of looking at student work collaboratively, a practice that many educators believe is at the heart of interschool collaboration and mutual improvement. It offers a strong collection of protocols, books, and other research materials, teacher-generated research based on student work, and links to other organizations that focus on student work.

National School Reform Faculty

Harmony Education Center
P.O. Box 1787
Bloomington, IN 47402
Voice: (812) 330-2702
Web: www.nsrfharmony.org

The National School Reform Faculty offers intensive professional development to educators and provides a structure for school people to work together in "critical friendship," looking closely at one another's practice and helping to improve and adapt it. A Critical Friends Group, the most common example, generally consists of six to ten school staff members who work together on a long-term basis with a focus on improving practice and increasing student learning. CFG members gather at least once a month for a two-to-three-hour meeting; they establish and publicly state learning goals for students, help each other think about more productive teaching practices, examine curriculum and student work, and identify school-culture and equity issues that affect student achievement.

School Design Organizations

Coalition of Essential Schools (ChangeLab site)

Web: www.changelab.org

School Redesign Network

Web: www.schoolredesign.net/srn/index.php

Community Organizing Organizations

Harwood Institute of Public Innovation

4915 St. Elmo Avenue, Suite 402
Bethesda, MD 20814
Voice: (301) 656-3669
Web: www.theharwoodinstitute.org

Public Education Network (PEN)

601 13th Street, NW, Suite 710 South
Washington, DC 20005
Voice: (202) 628-7460
Fax: (202) 628-1893
E-mail: pen@publiceducation.org
Web: www.publiceducation.org

PEN is a national association of seventy Local Education Funds—independent, non-profit, community-based organizations. LEFs are dedicated to increasing student achievement in public schools, especially among low-income, underserved students, and building support for high-quality public education. LEFs coordinate programs in a wide range of areas, and many focus on community-school partnerships. The PEN Web site is a fascinating look at local initiatives to improve schools and the lives of students, families, and teachers.

National Network of Partnership Schools

Johns Hopkins University
3003 N. Charles Street, Suite 200
Baltimore, MD 21218
Voice: (410) 516-8800
E-mail: nnps@csos.jhu.edu
Web: www.partnershipschools.org

The National Network of Partnership Schools is a group of nine hundred schools working to promote, evaluate, and improve their family and community partnership programs. In exchange for agreeing to a set of standards and practices for developing, implementing, and assessing their partnerships, schools gain access to training materials, workshops, and a newsletter. "Teachers Involve Parents in Schoolwork" is a particularly useful section of the group's Web site for educators interested in engaging families in students' daily academic efforts.

National Center for Family & Community Connections with Schools

Southwest Educational Development Laboratory
211 East Seventh Street
Austin, TX 78701-3253
Voice: (800) 476-6861
Fax: (512) 476-2286
E-mail: connections@sedl.org
Web: www.sedl.org/connections

Part of the Southwest Educational Development Laboratory, the National Center for Family & Community Connections with Schools produces research reports, holds conferences and satellite broadcasts, and maintains a Web site devoted to school-family-community partnerships. Its Resources section offers a searchable research database and a clear and comprehensive review and synthesis of research on school partnerships titled "A New Wave of Evidence: The Impact of School, Family, and Community Connections on Student Achievement."

Study Circles Resource Center

P.O. Box 203
697 Pomfret Street
Pomfret, CT 06258
Voice: (860) 928-2616
Fax: (860) 928-3713
E-mail: scrc@studycircles.org
Web: www.studycircles.org

The Study Circles Resource Center offers a process to create constructive conversation and action in one's community. In facilitated small group discussions, community members exchange views, generate solutions, and collaborate to transform their discussions into change. The Web site offers advice on organization, facilitation, and goal-setting along with other technical assistance, and offers success stories, links to local study circle programs, assessment and documentation information, and discussion guides focused on various civic issues including education. (For school-specific discussion structures, look for "Helping Every Student Succeed: Schools and Communities Working Together.")

Institute for Responsive Education

80 Prospect Street, 3rd Floor
Cambridge, MA 02138
Voice: (617) 873-0610
Web: www.responsiveeducation.org

For thirty years, the Institute for Responsive Education has distributed information, offered training and technical assistance, and worked as an advocate for effective school, family, and community partnerships. IRE's Web site defines what works best in school partnership programs at all grade levels and in various settings. It also presents IRE's past and ongoing research findings and links to its publications (some available free of charge). It also features a Tips section, which offers advice on starting and sustaining school-family-community partnerships in specific, one-page briefs.

Coalition for Community Schools

4455 Connecticut Avenue, NW, Suite 310
Washington, DC 20008
Voice: (202) 822-8405 ext. 156
Fax: (202) 872-4050
E-mail: ccs@iel.org
Web: www.communityschools.org

The Coalition for Community Schools promotes community schools that bring together services to support students, families, and community members. The group unites dozens of local, state, and national organizations as partners. Its Web site gathers resources from its partners and other useful sources to assist community school builders in the areas of research, design, advocacy, policy, and network building. The site also offers research reports, a large bibliography, and a diverse group of descriptions of community schools from around the country. These descriptions demonstrate a wide range of community school possibilities.

Family Involvement Network of Educators at the Harvard Family Research Project

3 Garden Street
Cambridge, MA 02138
Voice: (617) 495-9108
Fax: (617) 495-8594
E-mail: fine@gse.harvard.edu
Web: www.gse.harvard.edu/hfrp/index.html/

The Family Involvement Network of Educators provides resources to train teachers and families to work together. FINE publishes monthly research and resource updates and a semiannual electronic newsletter that concentrates on specific issues such as family involvement in mathematics or working with diverse communities. The Web site offers a large resource section with links to research, annotated bibliographies, course syllabi, teaching cases, and workshop materials.

Architecture

Reference

Duke, D. L., & Trautvetter, S. (2001). *Reducing the negative effects of large schools.* Washington, DC: National Clearinghouse for Educational Facilities.

Organizations

School Design Research Studio

Department of Engineering Professional Development

College of Engineering

University of Wisconsin-Madison

432 North Lake Street

Madison, WI 53706

E-mail: lackney@epd.engr.wisc.edu

Web: http://schoolstudio.engr.wisc.edu

Appendix D

Model Guidelines for Small Schools

In this section, we present guidelines for small schools that have been developed by three organizations that illustrate best practices and lessons learned in the field. These guidelines can be used in three ways. First, they can help schools begin to reflect and question their current practices and to focus their discussions on effective learning. Second, schools or design teams can discuss how each principle affects learning, use these principles to develop a vision of a new autonomous small school, and develop ways to deepen their practice in the school. Third, the guidelines can also be used as benchmarks from which schools can create indicators to assess and continually develop their practice.

The Common Principles of the Coalition of Essential Schools

1. The school should focus on helping young people learn to use their minds well. Schools should not be "comprehensive" if such a claim is made at the expense of the school's central intellectual purpose.

2. The school's goals should be simple: that each student master a limited number of essential skills and areas of knowledge. While these skills and areas will, to varying degrees, reflect the traditional academic disciplines, the program's design should be shaped by the intellectual and imaginative powers and competencies that the students need, rather than by "subjects" as conventionally defined. The aphorism "less is more" should dominate: curricular decisions should be guided by the aim of thorough student mastery and achievement rather than by an effort to merely cover content.

3. The school's goals should apply to all students, while the means to these goals will vary as those students themselves vary. School practice should be tailor-made to meet the needs of every group or class of students.

4. Teaching and learning should be personalized to the maximum feasible extent. Efforts should be directed toward a goal that no teacher have direct responsibility for more than 80 students in the high school and middle school and no more than 20 in the elementary school. To capitalize on this personalization, decisions about the details of the course of study, the use of students' and teachers' time, and the choice of teaching materials and specific pedagogies must be unreservedly placed in the hands of the principal and staff.

5. The governing practical metaphor of the school should be student-as-worker, rather than the more familiar metaphor of teacher-as-deliverer-of-instructional-services. Accordingly, a prominent pedagogy will be coaching, to provoke students to learn how to learn and thus to teach themselves.

6. Teaching and learning should be documented and assessed with tools based on student performance of real tasks. Students not yet at appropriate levels of competence should be provided intensive support and resources to assist them quickly to meet those standards. Multiple forms of evidence, ranging from ongoing observation of the learner to completion of specific projects, should be used to better understand the learner's strengths and needs, and to plan for further assistance. Students should have opportunities to exhibit their expertise before family and community. The diploma should be awarded upon a successful final demonstration of mastery for graduation—an "Exhibition." As the diploma is awarded when earned, the school's program proceeds with no strict age grading and with no system of credits earned by "time spent" in class. The emphasis is on the students' demonstration that they can do important things.

7. The tone of the school should explicitly and self-consciously stress values of unanxious expectation ("I won't threaten you but I expect much of you"), of trust (until abused), and of decency (the values of fairness, generosity, and tolerance). Incentives appropriate to the school's particular students and teachers should be emphasized. Parents should be key collaborators and vital members of the school community.

8. The principal and teachers should perceive themselves as generalists first (teachers and scholars in general education) and specialists second (experts in but one particular discipline). Staff should expect multiple

obligations (teacher-counselor-manager) and a sense of commitment to the entire school.

9. Ultimate administrative and budget targets should include, in addition to total student loads per teacher of 80 or fewer pupils on the high school and middle school levels and 20 or fewer on the elementary level, substantial time for collective planning by teachers, competitive salaries for staff, and an ultimate per pupil cost not to exceed that at traditional schools by more than 10 percent. To accomplish this, administrative plans may have to show the phased reduction or elimination of some services now provided students in many traditional schools.

10. The school should demonstrate nondiscriminatory and inclusive policies, practices, and pedagogies. It should model democratic practices that involve all who are directly affected by the school. The school should honor diversity and build on the strength of its communities, deliberately and explicitly challenging all forms of inequity.

The Bill & Melinda Gates Foundation's Attributes of High Achievement Schools

- *Common Focus:* The staff and students are focused on a few important goals. The school has adopted a consistent research-based instructional approach based on shared beliefs about teaching and learning. The use of time, tools, materials, and professional development activities are aligned with instruction.

- *High Expectations:* All staff members are dedicated to helping every student achieve state and local standards; all students are engaged in an ambitious and rigorous course of study; and all students leave school prepared for success in work, further education, and responsible citizenship.

- *Personalized:* The school is designed to promote powerful, sustained student relationships with adults where every student has an adult advocate and a personal plan for progress. Schools are small, intimate units of no more than 600 students (no more than 400 strongly recommended) so that staff and students can work closely together.

- *Respect and Responsibility:* The environment is authoritative, safe, ethical, and studious. The staff teaches, models, and expects responsible behavior and relationships based on mutual respect.

- *Time to Collaborate:* Staff has time to collaborate and develop skills and plans to meet the needs of all students. Parents are recognized as partners in education. Partnerships are developed with businesses for student work-based learning opportunities and with institutions of higher education to improve teacher preparation.

- *Performance Based:* Students are promoted to the next instructional level only when they have achieved competency; and students receive additional time and assistance when needed. Data-driven decisions shape a dynamic structure and schedule.

- *Technology as a Tool:* Teachers design engaging and imaginative curriculum linked to learning standards, they analyze results and have easy access to best practices and professional learning opportunities. Schools publish their progress and engage the community in dialogue about continuous improvement.

The School Redesign Network's Ten Features of Effective Small Schools

- *Personalization:* Smaller classes and reduced teacher pupil loads personalize learning.

- *Continuous relationships:* Advisory pairings and looping (when students and teachers stay together for multiple years) allow relationships to develop over time.

- *Standards and performance assessment:* Clear, high expectations and performance-based assessment help students learn.

- *Authentic curriculum:* Active, in-depth learning with real-world connections leads to higher achievement.

- *Adaptive pedagogy:* Successful teachers adjust their teaching modes to meet students where they are.

- *Antiracist teaching:* Democratic schools that seek out diversity provide a caring, respectful community for all students.

- *Qualified teachers:* Qualified teachers make a difference.

- *Collaboration and development:* Schools provide time for teachers to work together and develop their expertise.

- *Family and community connections:* Schools build relationships with families and communities to strengthen student learning.

- *Democratic decision making:* Shared governance allows for the creation of a common vision.

Appendix E

Plans, Processes, and Policies for a Conversion Strategy

Here is a detailed list of the tasks and decisions involved in a school conversion, sorted out by which ones require effort throughout the conversion process and which can be done once and allowed to stand. Feel free to photocopy it as a ready reference for the conversion team.

Continuing Tasks

Focus on building the capacity of individual educators, schools, and the district; planning of these tasks begins early in the conversion process and continues through the creation and growth of small autonomous schools.

Instructional Practice Professional Development

Identify how to support and structure opportunities for teachers to develop skills to teach effectively in the following areas of small school instruction. Questions to address:

- *Differentiated instruction:* How will teachers tailor curriculum and pedagogy to meet different skill levels, interests, and learning styles?

- *Heterogeneous grouping:* What instructional practices are effective in classrooms with students of different achievement levels?

- *Interdisciplinary curriculum:* How can teachers work with others to create curriculum across disciplines that maximizes student engagement and learning?

- *Project-based learning:* How will teachers emphasize learning activities that are long term, interdisciplinary, student-centered, and integrated with real-world issues and practices?

- *Block scheduling:* How will teachers use instructional learning blocks of varying lengths to meet learning and engagement goals?

- *Performance assessments:* How do teachers design and link demonstration of mastery to curriculum and pedagogy?

- *Service learning:* How will service learning (where students attend a range of off-campus sites) further learning objectives as students develop projects and skills in real-world environments and experiences?

- *Collaborative learning community:* What skills do teachers need to develop to take advantage of increased professional collaborative opportunities?

- *Advisories:* How will teachers be supported in facilitating advisories—consistent meetings with students to discuss individual and collective concerns not typically addressed in the classroom?

- *English language learner instructional plan:* How will the school develop schoolwide and classroom-specific plans to support English language learners? What skills do teachers need to possess to support ELL students?

- *Special education inclusion plan:* What schoolwide and classroom-specific plans will the school implement to appropriately identify and meet the needs of students with special needs? What skills do teachers need to develop to support special needs students?

Leadership

Establish a plan for identifying and developing new school leaders. Questions to address:

- *Develop teacher-leaders:* What practices will be implemented to cultivate teacher leadership and establish the distributive leadership structure that effective small schools need?

- *Large school leadership phase-out:* How will the large high school principal move out of that leadership role and into a new role when the small autonomous schools are opened?

- *Selecting and preparing administrators:* How will the skill set needed in new school leaders be identified? What strategies will be used to select and prepare leaders with the skills necessary for leading and managing a small autonomous high school? What strategies will be used to ensure new small school leaders have or acquire the necessary administrative credentials?

District Policy and Autonomies

Define how the district will reorganize itself and its relationship to schools to support the new educational mission, structure, culture, and instructional strategies of small autonomous schools. Questions to address:

- *District policies:* How will the district assess its policies and modify or create policies to best facilitate effective small schools?

- *Budget autonomy:* How will the schools control allocation of their resources so as to use them to create conditions that lead to sustained student learning? What district policies will ensure this autonomy?

- *Staffing autonomy:* How will the schools make decisions about hiring (and hire outside as well as from within the conversion school) to make sure staff have an educational philosophy that will support the new school mission? What district policies will ensure this autonomy?

- *Scheduling autonomy:* How will schools determine and structure their daily schedule (for both students and staff) to reach their specific instructional and professional development goals? What district policies will ensure this autonomy?

- *Curricular autonomy:* How will the schools' instructional philosophy guide the development of a curriculum and multiple assessments for student promotion and graduation that will carry out the school's educational mission? What district policies will ensure this autonomy, in contrast to imposing a district-mandated curriculum?

- *Governance autonomy:* How will each school select its own leadership (one or more principals or directors) and governing council? What district policies will ensure this autonomy?

- *Teacher credentials:* How will the district support teachers in getting credentials that may be necessary to work in small schools?

- *Waivers versus policies:* What is the best route to create and institutionalize policies that make small schools sustainable?

- *Accountability practices:* What accountability structure will ensure that schools are successful and effective and maintain necessary autonomies?

Community Engagement

What role do you see various stakeholders playing in the planning of the conversion and the development of small schools? What strategies will your conversion effort implement to communicate with and engage stakeholders effectively? Questions to address:

- *Communications plan:* How will the conversion effort communicate what is going to happen, accept feedback, address issues, plan community forums, and address other communication needs?

- *Design teams:* Will the efforts require that design teams include community members?

- *Partnerships:* In what ways will the conversion effort partner with local community groups and organizations?

Discrete Tasks

These tasks are specific to the conversion process. Once they are implemented, they do not occur again.

Roll-Out Plans

Create a plan for the roll-out, or phasing, of new school designs and openings that will maximize the creation of successful and sustainable small schools. Questions to address:

- *Number and range of schools:* How many schools are necessary for a district? The goal is to create a comprehensive system of small schools with a variety of distinct options in which every student has access to every learning environment and a range of environments to meet the needs of each student. What similarities and differences do you envision in the character and size of each small school?

- *Size of schools:* Based on the needs of the students the small schools will serve and the instructional goals of the schools, what is an appropriate size for the different schools that will open?

- *Large school phase-out:* How and when will the comprehensive high school be closed?

- *Location of schools:* If there are options, what locations maximize success for creating successful, sustainable small schools?

- *Timing of school openings:* How will efforts provide the greatest chance of creating successful, sustainable small schools while offering the best education to the most students as quickly as possible?

- *Grade levels at opening:* What grades should be included in the opening of new schools, to best balance the priorities of meeting the needs of all students and of creating sustainable, effective small schools?

School Vision and Identity

The school's overall purpose and organizing framework for how the school is going to teach students and improve the learning practice or process. Questions to address:

- *Individual school missions and visions:* What are the vision and mission of your proposed school conversion and your intended outcomes and goals for students? What is your school's instructional philosophy? How does your school believe that students learn, access, and incorporate new knowledge? What research supports your philosophy?

- *Design vision-driven school:* How is your anticipated school design linked to your overall mission, instructional philosophy, and your intended student outcomes?

- *School culture:* Recognizing that a strong school culture is pivotal and that conversion entails transformation of existing school culture, how will the conversion process ensure that each school has a distinct culture, grounded in common values, that supports its mission and instructional goals?

Curricular Identity

Establish a curricular identity that prepares all students for higher education, work, and citizenship. Questions to address:

- *Create a powerful curriculum that prepares all students for college:* How will the school facilitate the development of each child with personalization and academic rigor? What approach will the school take to choosing or designing curriculum in math and other subjects?

- *Sharing resources (or not):* What curricular resources can be shared among interconnected schools without weakening each school's instructional focus and vision?

- *Curricular breadth and depth:* How will schools create a personalized rather than comprehensive curriculum?

Teacher Assignment

How will existing teachers be reassigned within the new small schools? Will there be recruitment of new teachers from outside the conversion school?

Student Assignment

How will existing students be reassigned within the new small schools? How do assignment and choice plans account for differences in students by ethnicity, sex, and learning needs?

Sharing a Building

Interconnected schools function most effectively when they come to agreements about how to work together, share facilities, and solve and negotiate issues that arise. Questions to address:

- *Facilities manager, Building Council:* Will there be a Building Council or a manager (or both) to oversee communal functions and space within a shared facility?

- *Decision-making process:* What will be an agreed-upon process for coming to acceptable decisions?

- *Creating unique space:* What unique and common facilities and space do you anticipate that the small schools will require?

- *Physical layout:* How will separate space with distinct boundaries be created for the new schools? What autonomies in terms of space will be granted to each small school?

- *Shared expectations (discipline):* How will interconnected schools create a shared set of rules and expectations to ensure that students will be treated fairly by all schools? Each school wants to ensure that its students are treated well by the other schools, that its rules are respected by the other schools, and that its efforts to create a new culture are not undermined.

- *Shared accountability:* How will schools create a sense of mutual accountability in that people feel a sense of responsibility to one another and to the larger school community.

The Harwood Institute's Principles of Civic Engagement

If you are engaged in a small school conversion effort, following these principles will make things go more smoothly every step of the way.

Pursue Civic Engagement, Not Public Input

Often, we make the mistake of thinking that if we give people the chance to speak, we have participated in an engagement effort. Merely listening to the voices of individuals does not provide the context necessary to understand the complexity of an issue, or provide a coherent picture of how to move forward.

In pursuing input, we often:

- Ask each person to give their individual view and quickly—"Please line up at the microphone in front and you have 30 seconds."

- Believe that when we "add up" everyone's responses, we now know what people believe.

- Set up goals to get as many people as possible to speak: credibility is gained through numbers.

- Focus on what people "think."

Engagement:

- Requires give and take between and among people.

- Requires time.

- Takes people considering different perspectives and points of view and the weighing of choices and trade-offs.

- Produces public knowledge about what people hold valuable, aspirations, common purpose, directions for action, who will do what.

- Works from the assumption that we each hold self-interests but have the capacity (and desire) to act as citizens.

Engage People as Citizens, Not Consumers

Schools and other public institutions often adopt the mindset of customer service when communicating with the public. By attempting to cater to the needs of each individual, they often lose sight of the community. Such an approach can actually push people away from the process by making them feel that they have nothing to contribute to the effort.

When we think of people as consumers we often:

- Inflate people's desire to think about their own self-interest—crowding out room to find common interests.

- See everyone as a "customer"—which can lead people to make demands, turn them into claimants.

- Back away from challenging people to think beyond themselves and those immediately around them.

- Ask people repeatedly the question: "What can I do for you?"

As citizens, people have the capacity to:

- Hold self-interest but also care about the world around them—see beyond just themselves.

- Weigh different perspectives, choices, and trade-offs—and, when the conditions are right, seek to do so.

- Take on challenges, and even enjoy the tension it brings, and see possibilities from it—"For once, we're trying to do something."

Discover Voices, Not Simply Demographics

One of the greatest temptations when planning to engage the public is to develop a marketing campaign designed to target specific groups, based on preconceived notions and stereotypes. Such an approach undercuts an engagement effort, and drowns out people's voices.

When seeking to "find" people to engage, we often use a demographic lens:

- Pull out Census numbers and make sure we get to all the groups.
- Assume that "each group" has a different opinion and is different.
- Analyze the results first by demographic.

An alternative is to use something like the following lens:

- Make sure to include people—all people; for instance, official leaders and "ordinary citizens."
- Be open to the idea that people may hold similar "voices" (perspectives, aspirations) across demographic lines—changing who you need to engage and why.
- Analyze the results first and foremost around substance, not demographics.

Seek Common Ground, Not Consensus

The ultimate goals of engagement efforts are not to reach consensus, but rather to explore the values that each participant brings to the table that informs their positions on specific issues. It is through this approach to engagement that we make progress where before there were only roadblocks.

Say to a group of people, "We're here to build consensus" and:

- They believe they must come to agree on (nearly) everything they are discussing.

- They water down issues, avoid real tensions, seek compromise, go to the lowest common denominator—all in search of "consensus."

- People believe if they don't agree with everything, then they can't be part of what is happening.

Watch a group seeking common ground and:

- The test is: "can I live with this?" I may not agree with everything, but overall, I can stay at the table.

- The underlying assumption is that people share common aspirations, and on most issues, there is much more agreement than disagreement——the goal is to uncover that.

- Common ground is about seeking and seeing possibilities, asking: "What if . . ."

Provide Knowledge, Not More Information

Information overload often leads to people retreating from an engagement process. Illuminating connections in the web of information that people already possess helps them gain knowledge about the situation, and provides the foundation on which to build conversations.

When people don't know something, we see them as uninformed—so we:

- Rush out and give people tons of information.

- Seek to "educate people" often forgetting that they too know some things—as if they'd respond better if only they knew more.

- Frame information as if people are islands unto themselves: "News you can use."

- Treat people as "passive recipients"—seldom asking them to think about, process, see, and connect things; the result of which is people stay disconnected and make demands or act as claimants.

What if we thought more about the idea that people seek knowledge; then, for instance, we:

- Recognize that people are seeking to understand and make sense of the world around them—to gain context and perspective, create coherence.

- Illuminate ambiguities and uncertainty and risk—with the goal of helping people gain clarity of complex issues.

- Provide people with the essential facts: help connect fragments of information—which leads to relevance, meaning, and engagement.

- See people as part of the community—and, thus, needing certain kinds of knowledge, not only for themselves, but also to make common decisions.

References

Allen, L., & Sternberg, A. (2004). *Big buildings, small schools: Using a small schools strategy for high school reform.* Boston, MA: Jobs for the Future.

American Institutes for Research & SRI International. (2003). *The National School District and Network Grants Program: Year 1 evaluation report.* Palo Alto, CA: Author.

American Institutes for Research & SRI International. (2004). *The National School District and Network Grants Program: Year 2 evaluation report.* Palo Alto, CA: Author.

Ancess, J. (2003). *Beating the odds: High schools as communities of commitment.* New York: Teachers College Press.

Ancess, J., & Wichterle, S. (1999). *How the Coalition Campus Schools have reimagined high school: Seven years later.* New York: NCREST, Teachers College, Columbia University.

Bernhardt, V. (1994). *The school portfolio.* Princeton Junction, NJ: Eye on Education.

The Bill & Melinda Gates Foundation. (n.d.). Problems with large, impersonal high schools. Available online: http://www.gatesfoundation.org/Education/ ResearchAndEvaluation/Evaluation/RelatedInfo/MakingCaseForSmallSchools .htm. Access date: June 13, 2005.

Boston Public Schools. (2003). *Request for proposal for 2003–2004 Pilot Schools.* Boston: Author.

Boston Public Schools & Center for Collaborative Education. (2000). *The Boston Pilot Schools school self-study guide.* Boston: Author.

Bryk, A. S., & Thum, Y. M. (1989, Fall). The effects of high school organization on dropping out: An exploratory investigation. *American Educational Research Journal, 26,* 353–383.

Center for Collaborative Education. (2002). *How Pilot Schools use freedom over staffing, scheduling, and budget to meet student needs.* Boston: Author.

Center for Collaborative Education. (2004). *How are Boston Pilot Schools faring? An analysis of student demographics, engagement, and performance.* Boston: Author.

Center for the Future of Teaching and Learning. (2000). *The status of the teaching profession 2000: An update to the Teaching and California's Future task force.* Santa Cruz, CA: Author.

Civil Rights Project at Harvard University. (2002). *Discrimination in special education.* Cambridge, MA: Author.

Cotton, K. (1996). *School size, school climate, and student performance. Close-Up #20.* Portland, OR: Northwest Regional Educational Laboratory.

Cotton, K. (2001, December). *New small learning communities: Findings from recent literature.* Portland, OR: Northwest Regional Educational Laboratory.

Cushman, K. (1999, November). How small schools increase student learning (and what large schools can do about it). *Principal, 79*(2), 20–22.

Darling-Hammond, L. (1997). *The right to learn: A blueprint for creating schools that work.* San Francisco: Jossey-Bass.

Darling-Hammond, L., Ancess, J., McGregor, K., & Zuckerman, D. (2000). *Inching toward reform in New York City: The Coalition campus schools project.* In E. Clinchy (Ed.), *Creating new schools: How small schools are changing American education* (pp. 163–181). New York: Teachers College Press.

Darling-Hammond, L., Ancess, J., & Ort, S. (2002, Fall). Reinventing high school: An analysis of the Coalition Campus Schools Project. *American Educational Research Journal, 39*(3), 639–673.

DuFour, R., & Eaker, R. E. (1998). *Professional learning communities at work: Best practices for enhancing student achievement.* Bloomington, IN: National Education Service.

Elmore, R. (2000). *Building a new structure for school leadership.* Washington, DC: Albert Shanker Institute.

Elmore, R. (2002). Beyond instructional leadership: Hard questions about practice. *Educational Leadership, 59*(8), 22–25.

Evans, R. (1996). *The human side of school change: Reform, resistance, and the real-life problems of innovation.* Jossey-Bass: San Francisco.

Fairtest. (n.d.). A call for an authentic state-wide assessment system. Available online: http://www.fairtest.org/care/accountability.html. Access date: April 23, 2005.

Fine, M. (1998). Introduction: What's so good about small schools? In (Ed., Michelle Fine & Jan Sommerville) *Small schools, big imaginations: A creative look at urban public schools,* pp. 2–13. Chicago: Cross City Campaign for School Reform.

Flaxman, L. (2004). Interview with Anna Le, Life Academy graduate. *Horace, 20*(3), 5.

Fullan, M. (2001). *Leading in a culture of change.* Jossey-Bass: San Francisco.

Gates Education Policy Paper. (2003). *Closing the graduation gap: Toward high schools that prepare all students for college, work, and citizenship.* Seattle, WA: Bill & Melinda Gates Foundation.

Gladden, R. (1998). The small school movement: A review of the literature. In M. Fine & J. Somerville (Eds.), *Small schools, big imaginations: A creative look at urban public schools,* pp. 113–137. Chicago: Cross City Campaign for Urban School Reform.

Greene, J., & Forster, G. (2003). *Public high school graduation and college readiness rates in the United States.* New York: Manhattan Institute.

Gregory, T. (2001). Breaking up large high schools: Five common (and understandable) errors of execution. ERIC Digest. Charleston, WV: ERIC Clearinghouse on Rural Education and Small Schools. (ED 459 049).

Harwood Institute of Public Innovation. (2002). *Public engagement and small schools conversation guide.* Bethesda, MD: Harwood Institute of Public Innovation.

Hawley-Miles, K., and Darling-Hammond, L. (1997). Rethinking the Allocation of Teaching Resources: Some Lessons from High Performing Schools. *Developments in School Finance,* pp. 31–58. Available online: http://nces.ed.gov/pubs98/dev97/98212e.asp. Access date: June 21, 2005.

Howley, C., Strange, M., & Bickel, R. (2000). Research about school size and school performance in impoverished communities. ERIC Digest. Charleston, WV: ERIC Clearinghouse on Rural Education and Small Schools. (ED 448 968).

Klonsky, S., & Klonsky, M. (1999, September). Countering anonymity through small schools. *Educational Leadership, 57*(1), 38–41.

Kotter, J. (1996). *Leading change.* Boston: Harvard Business School Press.

Lambert, L. (2002). A framework for shared leadership. *Educational Leadership, 59*(8), 37–40.

Lashway, L. (1998–1999). School size: Is small better? *Research Roundup, 15*(2), entire issue.

Lear, R. (2004, April). *Conversions in urban, suburban, and rural communities: What we are learning.* Paper presented at the Annual Meeting of the American Educational Research Association, San Diego, CA.

Lee, V. E., & Loeb, S. (2000, Spring). School size in Chicago elementary schools: Effects on teachers' attitudes and students' achievement. *American Educational Research Journal, 37*(1), 3–32.

Lee, V. E., Smith, J., & Croninger, R. G. (1995, Fall). Another look at high school restructuring: More evidence that it improves student achievement, and more insight into why. *Issues in Restructuring Schools, 7,* 1–10.

Monk, D. H. (1987). School District Enrollment and Inequality in the Supply of Classes. *Economics of Education Review, 6*(4), 365–377.

Mortenson, T. (2000). NCES-IPEDS graduation rate survey. *Postsecondary Education Opportunity.* Available online: http://www.postsecondary.org/.

Mortenson, T. (2001, October). High school graduation rate by family income quartile for dependent 18–24-year-olds. (Graph.) *Postsecondary Education Opportunity.* Available online: http://www.postsecondary.org/.

Nieto, S. (2000). A gesture toward justice: Small schools and the promise of equal education. In W. Ayers, M. Klonsky, & G. Lyon (Eds.), *A simple justice: The challenge of small schools.* New York: Teachers College Press.

O'Neil, J. (1995/1996). On tapping the power of school-based management: A conversation with Michael Strembitsky. *Educational Leadership, 53*(4), 66–70.

Raywid, M. A. (1996). *The movement to create mini-schools, schools-within-schools, and separate small schools.* ERIC Digest. New York: ERIC Clearinghouse on Urban Education. (ED 396 045).

Raywid, M. A. (1999). *Current literature on small schools.* ERIC Digest. Charleston, WV: ERIC Clearinghouse on Rural Education and Small Schools. (ED 425 049).

Raywid, M., & Schmerler, G. (2003). *Not so easy going: The policy environments of small urban schools and schools-within-schools.* ERIC Digest. Charleston, WV: ERIC Clearinghouse on Rural Education and Small Schools. (ED 474 653).

Roellke, C. (1996, December). Curriculum Adequacy and Quality in High Schools Enrolling Fewer Than 400 Pupils (9–12). ERIC Digest. Charleston, WV: ERIC Clearinghouse on Rural Education and Small Schools. (ED 401 090).

Sarason, S. B. (1991). *The predictable failure of educational reform: Can we change course before it's too late?* San Francisco: Jossey-Bass.

Schlechty, P. (2001). *Shaking up the schoolhouse.* San Francisco: Jossey-Bass.

Schoggen, P., & Schoggen, M. (1988). Student voluntary participation and high school size. *Journal of Educational Research, 81*(5), 288–293.

School Redesign Network. (2002). *Ten features of good small schools.* Palo Alto, CA: School of Education, Stanford University.

Senge, P. M. (1990). *The fifth discipline: The art and practice of the learning organization.* New York: Currency Doubleday.

Senge, P. M., Cambron-McCabe, N., Lucas, T., Smith, B., & Dutton, J. (2000). *Schools that learn: A fifth discipline fieldbook for educators, parents, and everyone who cares about education.* New York: Currency Doubleday.

Small Schools Project. (2003a). Things you can count on happening. *Learning Network Newsletter, 1*(2), 1–2, 4.

Small Schools Project. (2003b). Values guide student placement decisions. *Learning Network Newsletter, 7*(1), 1, 4.

U.S. Census Bureau. (2002). *The big payoff: Educational attainment and synthetic estimates of work-life earnings.* Washington, DC: U.S. Census Bureau.

U.S. Department of Education. (2001). *An overview of smaller learning communities in high schools.* Washington, DC: Office of Elementary and Secondary Education and the Office of Vocational and Adult Education.

Wagner, T. (2001). Leadership for learning: An action theory of school change. *Phi Delta Kappan, 82*(5), 378–383.

Warner-King, K., & Price, M. (2004). *Legal issues and small high schools: Strategies to support innovation in Washington State.* Seattle: Center on Reinventing Public Education, University of Washington.

Wasley, P. A., & Lear, R. J. (2001, March). Small schools, real gains. *Educational Leadership, 58*(6), 22–27.

Wasley, P., Fine, M., Gladden, M., Holland, N. E., King, S. P., Mosak, E., & Powell, L. (2000). *Small schools: Great strides: A study of new small schools in Chicago.* New York: Bank Street College of Education.

West Clermont Local School District. (2001). *Creating the high schools we need.* Cincinnati, OH: Author.

Index

A

Accountability, 10, 47–50
Adams County, Colorado, 14–16
Adaptive pedagogy, 88
Administrators. *See* Stakeholders
Advanced Placement (AP) courses, 24, 105–106
Alberta, Canada, 42
Allen, L., 135
The American High School Today (Conant), ix
American Institutes for Research & SRI International,
    12, 43, 136, 138
Ancess, J., 10, 50
Anderson, M., 87
Annenburg Institute for School Reform, 49
Apprenticeship, 77
Arts Academy, 132
Assessment, 39, 87
Assignment policy: for students, 80, 123, 129–131,
    135–140; for teachers, 148–152
Athens, Ohio, 94
Attendance policies, 39
Autonomy, 4, 38–41
Ayers, W., xi

B

Baron, D., 99, 133
Bay Area Coalition for Equitable Schools (BayCES):
    autonomy and, 38, 43; community involvement and,
    61, 62; leadership and, 93, 100–101; parent involve-
    ment and, 66
Benson, M., 66–67, 128–129
Bernhardt, V., 22
Bickel, R., 10
"Big bang" approach, to new school openings, 123–124
Big Picture Company, 77
Big Picture High Schools, 32
Bill & Melinda Gates Foundation: design process
    and, 30; district policies and, 43; and failure of com-
    prehensive high schools, 7; and features of small

autonomous schools, 83; and objectives for students,
    12; school size and, 131; start-up costs and, 53; stu-
    dent assignment policy and, 136
Block schedule, 86, 87
Bloomington, Indiana, 133
Boston Arts Academy, 4, 78–79
Boston Pilot Schools, 38–39, 45, 48–50, 53
Boston Public Schools, 11, 39, 41, 45, 49, 53
Breaking Ranks, 30
Breaking Ranks II, 30
Bronx Academy of Visual Arts, 127
Bronx High School for the Visual Arts, 72–73, 110
Bronx International High School, 15, 80, 108, 139, 140
Bronx New Century High Schools, 8, 72
Brookhaven High School, 107–108, 129, 130
Brown, S., 15, 77, 132
Brown University, 30
Bryk, A. S., 10
Budget issues, 38, 39, 44–46
Building Council, 33, 112–114, 116, 117
Building, sharing of. *See* Facility-sharing issues
Businesses. *See* Stakeholders
Buy-in, 60

C

Calendar, 38–39
California Tomorrow, 80
Cambron-McCabe, N., 18
Career-based schools, 76–77
Carnegie Institute, ix
Carve-out approach, to school location, 122, 128
CBO (community-based organization), 62, 64
Center for Applied Special Technology, 88
Center for Collaborative Education, xi, 10, 40, 41, 45,
    49, 100–101
Center for the Future of Teaching and Learning, 6
Center of Strength, 20, 62, 63–65
Central Park East Secondary School, 92
Certification, 147, 148

CES. *See* Coalition of Essential Schools (CES)

CFG (critical friends group training), 89

Chicago, Illinois, 74, 76–77, 94, 128

Choice, and small autonomous schools, 135–140, 149

Choices Preparatory Academy, 132

Christopher Columbus High School, 127

Ciancio, C., 14–16, 18, 44, 145, 146

Cincinnati, Ohio, 8, 74–76, 95

Civil Rights Project, 78

Clover Park High School, 80–81, 85, 106

Co-housing, 122, 126

Coalition of Essential Schools (CES), xi, 4, 29–30, 32, 102

Collaboration, and conversion process, 63–65

College readiness: as goal of high school, 13, 24, 60, 77, 92; measures to ensure, 105

Columbus High School, 72–73, 113

Columbus, Ohio, 107–108, 129, 130

Common Principles, of Coalition of Essential Schools, 29–30, 32, 102

Commonwealth charter schools, 48

Communications/marketing plan, 30

Community-based organization (CBO), 62, 64

Community involvement. *See* Stakeholders

Comprehensive high schools, 7, 103–105

Conant, J. B., ix

Conditional certification, 147

Contiguous space, 111–112

Contractual concerns, 145–149

Controlled choice, 138–140, 149

Conversion: district transformation and, 33; guiding principles of, 12–13; of infrastructure, 11–12; phases of, 16–20, 21, 25–36; process of, 5, 60–68; strategic planning and, 20–23; summary of phases in, 26–27; underlying beliefs and, 23–25

Cotton, K., 10, 11

Counseling teachers out, 148–149

Creaming, 139

Credentialing, for small school leaders, 98, 99

Critical friends group (CFG) training, 89

Cross-over classes, 106–109

Cross-school approach, to student access, 129–130

Curriculum: advanced placement alternatives and, 105–106; cross-over classes and, 106–109; district and, 44; electives and, 103–105; school identity and, 10, 73, 76–77, 104; small school success and, 39; and universal design for learning, 88

Cushman, K., 10

D

Darling-Hammond, L., 10, 30, 38, 40, 50

Decision-making process, and facility-sharing issues, 112–115

Demographics, and student assignment policy, 139–140

Denver, Colorado, 138

Design of small autonomous schools, 21, 25–36, 84–86

Design teams, 64, 66–68, 150

Differentiated instruction, 24

Discipline policies, 39

Discovery Academy, 132

Distributive model of leadership, 93–95, 96, 99, 145

District: accountability and, 47–50; budget autonomy and, 44–46; curriculum and, 44; new roles for, 33, 41–43; waivers and, 50–51, 52

District staff. *See* Stakeholders

Diversity, 4–5, 104

Dropout rates, 105

Dual certification, 148

Dual enrollment program, 105

DuFour, R., 44

Dutton, J., 18

E

Eaker, R. E., 44

East Cleveland, Ohio, 15, 57, 62, 77, 132

East Side House Settlement, 65

Edmonton Public Schools, 42

Educational Alliance, at Brown University, 30

Electives, 103–105

Elementary school students, 125, 127, 130–131

ELL. *See* English language learners (ELL)

Elmore, R., 15–16, 91

Emergency certification, 147

Endorsement-related assignment, 147

Engagement phase, of conversion, 16–20

English language learners (ELL), 79–80, 86, 88–89, 140–141

Enrollment number, 4

Entrepreneurship High School, 74, 94

Equity, 6, 80, 135–136, 138

Evaluation, 10, 47–50

Evans, R., 18

Expectations, and facility sharing, 115–116

Expeditionary Learning, 32

Experience Academy, 132

Exploration phase, of conversion, 16–20

F

Facility-sharing issues, 110–117

Faculty size, 92

Fairtest, 48, 49

Federal Hocking High School, 94

Fenway High School, 11, 41, 79, 104

Fenway Institute for Urban School Renewal, 100–101

Fine, M., xi, 10, 83

Flaxman, L., 67, 68

Forster, G., 4

Foster High School, 132

Fremont Educational Complex, 66

Fremont High School, 66, 67

French, D., 40

Fullan, M., 18

Futures protocol, 85

G

Garfin, G., 113, 114–115

Gates, B. *See* Bill & Melinda Gates Foundation

Gates Education Policy Paper, 3
GCRTA (Greater Cleveland Regional Transit Authority), 62–64
Gender equity, 139
Gerstein, B., 74, 94
Gladden, R., 10
Glen Este High School, 95
Global Enterprise Academy, 127
Governance, and small autonomous school success, 39
Grade levels, in small autonomous schools, 123, 128–129
Graduation requirements, 39
Greater Cleveland Regional Transit Authority (GCRTA), 62–64
Greene, J., 4
Gregory, T., 11

H

Hanson, H., 73, 81, 85
Harmony School, 133
Hart, B., 9, 86–87
Harvard University, 78
Harwood Institute of Public Innovation, 56–57, 62, 63
Hawley-Miles, K., 38, 40
Heisler, D., 133
Heterogeneous classrooms, 87–89
Hierarchical model of leadership, 93–95
"Highly qualified" requirements, of No Child Left Behind Act, 146–148
Honors courses, 24
Honts, F., 87
Hothousing, 53, 122, 125, 126
HOUSSE (high, objective, uniform state standard of evaluation), 147
Howey, M., 65
Howley, C., 10
Humble, Texas, 152

I

Identity, of small autonomous schools, 10, 73, 76–77, 104
Implementation phase, and conversion, 33–36
Indianapolis, Indiana, 25, 47, 65, 99, 145
Information Age, requirements of, 8
Instruction, and small autonomous schools, 10, 30, 44, 60–61, 82–90, 148
Integration, of new staff, 151–152
Intellectual vibrancy, 6
Intercession, use of, 104
Interconnected schools. *See* Facility-sharing issues
Internships, 105

J

Jamentz, K., 84
Jobs for the Future, 77, 135
John F. Kennedy High School, 85–86
Julia Richman Complex, 5, 125, 130–131

K

Kennedy, M., 8, 95, 96, 145
Klonsky, M., 10, 76–77

Klonsky, S., 10
KnowledgeWorks Foundation: Center of Strength and, 63–64; community involvement and, 53, 61, 62; and design phase of conversion, 25; and designing effective schools, 30; exploration process and, 20, 21; leadership training and, 100–101; and student enrollment numbers, 4; timing of school opening and, 124
Kotter, J., 18
Kozol, J., 7

L

LaGuardia Middle College High, 4–5
Lakewood, Washington, 80–81, 85, 106
Lambert, L., 95
Lashway, L., 10
LEAD (Leading for Equity, Achievement and Democracy), 93, 100–101
Leadership, and small autonomous schools, 18–20, 91–101, 145
Leading for Equity, Achievement and Democracy (LEAD), 93, 100–101
Lear, R. J., 10, 131
Lee, V. E., 10
Lehman High School, 133
Leominster High School, 9, 86–87
Leominster, Massachusetts, 9, 86–87, 98
Life Academy, 67
Literacy plan, 30
Location, of small autonomous schools, 122, 125–128
Loeb, S., 10
Looping, 40
Lott, A., 63, 64
Low-income students, 6, 7, 66
Lucas, T., 18
Lump sum budgets, 45

M

Management, leadership vs., 92–93
Manhattan International High School, 139
Manual High School, 138
Mapleton Public Schools, 14–16, 18, 32, 44, 126
Marble Hill School for International Studies, 80, 85–86
Marketing plan, 30
Math, Science, and Technology Academy (MAST), 8, 95, 145
McGregor, K., 50
Meier, D., xi, 92
Memorandum of Understanding (MOU), 19, 51, 52, 65
Met School, 4, 32
Middle College High School, 105
Middle school students, 125, 127, 130–131
Modified controlled choice, 139
Monk, D. H., 104
Morris High School, 108
Mortenson, T., 3, 4
Mott Haven Preparatory High School, 65
Multi-level buildings, 122, 127
Myatt, L., 11, 23–24, 92

N

Nadelstern, E., 37, 42–43, 64, 84
National Association of Secondary School Principals, 30
National School District and Network Grants Program: Year 2 Evaluation Report, 138
National School Reform Faculty, 99, 133
New England Small Schools Network, 139
New York City, 4–5, 8, 11, 15, 51, 61, 64, 80, 85–86
Nieto, S., 9
No Child Left Behind Act, 146–148
Northeastern University, 100–101

O

Oakland (California) Unified School District, 42–43, 46, 62, 66–67, 128–129
Oakland Community Organizations (OCO), 62, 67
Olsen, L., 80
O'Neil, J., 42
Open approach, to school formation, 80–81
Open choice, 138
Ort, S., 10
Out-of-endorsement assignment waivers, 147

P

Pablo Neruda Academy for Architecture and World Studies, 133
Parent Congress, 66
Parent Welcome Center, 63
Parental notification, and teacher assignment, 148
Parents. *See* Stakeholders
Partnership Center, 66
Partnerships, and conversion process, 63–65
Path of Public Knowledge, 57.
Pedagogy. *See* Instruction, and small autonomous schools
Pelham Preparatory Academy, 127
Performance assessment, 39, 87
Personalization, 6, 10, 87–89, 103–105
Phased approach, to new school openings, 124
Pilot School Network, 49
Pilot Schools, in Boston, 38–39, 45, 48–50, 53
Planning, and conversion, 20–23, 30
Policy changes, 39, 50–51
Political pressure, and conversion process, 62
Poor students, 6, 7, 66
Portfolio process, 105
Postsecondary education preparation. *See* College readiness
The Power of Their Ideas (Meier), xi
Preparatory structures, for small autonomous schools, 123, 133
Price, M., 51, 52, 146–148
Principal Residency Network (PRN), 100–101
Principals: facility-sharing issues and, 112–115; leadership and, 98; selection of, 39, 92–93
Professional development, 86–87, 89–90, 144
Promotion requirements, 39
Providence, Rhode Island, 4, 32

Public Engagement and Small Schools Conversation Guide (Harwood Institute), 63
Public sector organizations. *See* Stakeholders

Q

Quest High School, 152

R

Random teacher assignment, 150
Ratio, of students, 4
Raymond, M., 124
Raywid, M. A., xiii, 10, 148
Real-world learning, 77
Reeder, J., 87
Request for Proposals (RFP) process, 28–29, 130
Resources, 52–54, 106–109
Roellke, C., 109

S

Sarason, S. B., 23, 155
Schlechty, P., 9
Schmerler, G., 148
Schoettlin, H., 152–153
Schoggen, M., 104
Schoggen, P., 104
School board. *See* Stakeholders
School-by-school approach, to student access, 129
School calendar, 38–39
School district. *See* District
School for World Studies, 145
School of Creative Arts and Design, 145
School of Entrepreneurship, Finance, and Transportation, 64
School of Environmental Studies, 5
School of Technology and Communications, 75–76
School of the Arts High School, 128
School Portfolio, 22
School quality review (SQR), 48, 49–50
School Redesign Network (SRN), 30, 83, 88
School size, 123, 131–132
Schwarz, P., 100–101
Scott-George, K., 42, 46
SeaTac, Washington, 35
Seattle, Washington, 73
Seeding, 122, 125, 126–127
Selection, of leaders, 96–100
Self-determination, and small autonomous schools, 10
Senge, P. M., 17, 18, 60, 61
Senior exhibition, 105
Senior Exit Action, 145
Seniority rights, of teachers, 148
Shapiro, S., 107
Shared resources, 106–109
Shaw High School, 15, 57, 62–63, 77, 132
Sheltered school concept, 127
Silverman, M., 124
Size issues, 4, 92, 123, 131–132
Sizer, T., xi, 6, 102
Skyview High School, 14, 126

Small autonomous schools, elements of, 5–6, 10, 21, 83
Small learning communities, 11, 52–53, 133, 150
Small School Project Coach Collective, 73
Small school strategic plan, 30
Small Schools Policy, in Oakland, 62
Small Schools Program, 136
Small Schools Project, 36, 131, 137
Small Schools Workshop, 76–77
Smith, B., 18
Smith, J., 10
South Bronx, New York, 65
South Shore High School, 74, 94
Space constraints, and facility sharing, 116–117
Space requirements, 40
Special education students, 78–79, 140–141
Specialist teachers, 152–153
Spring, S., 100
Sputnik launch, ix
SQR (school quality review), 48, 49–50
St. Paul, Minnesota, 5
Staffing issues, 39, 44–46
Stakeholders: conversion and, 16–25; early engagement of, 55–60; leadership and, 95; and ownership of conversion process, 60–68
Stanford University, 30, 88
Start-up costs, 52–54
Steinberg, P., 8, 64–65, 72
Sternberg, A., 135
Strange, M., 10
Students: assignment policy and, 80, 123, 129–131, 135–140; of color, 6, 7, 66; conversion process and, 65–68
Summary: of conversion process, 26–27; of processes, policies, documents in new school, 34–35
Suransky, S., 15, 108–109, 114, 115, 140

T

Teachers: assignment strategies for, 148–152; leadership and, 94–95, 96, 145; and No Child Left Behind Act requirements, 146–148; outside interests and, 144–145; professional development and, 86–87, 89–90, 144; and specialist teachers, 152–153; unions and, 51–52, 53, 148. *See also* Stakeholders
Teaching practice. *See* Instruction, and small autonomous schools
Team teaching, 148
Teams, for design phase, 28–29
Theme, and small autonomous schools, 72, 73, 76–77
Thomas Proctor High School, 100, 139–140
Thum, Y. M., 10
Timing, of new school openings, 122, 123–124

Tracking, avoidance of, 136
Training programs, for small school leaders, 100–101
Transition phase, and conversion, 32–33
Tyee High School, 35, 54, 124
Tytler, P., 106

U

UDL (universal design for learning), 88
Underlying beliefs/assumptions, and conversion, 23–25
Unions, and teachers, 51–52, 53, 148
United Federation of Teachers, 51, 148
Universal design for learning (UDL), 88
U.S. Census Bureau, 4
U.S. Department of Education, 11, 52–53
Utica, New York, 100, 139–140

V

Vander Ark, T., 83
Vision phase, of conversion, 16–20
Vision statement, 71–76, 80–81
Vocational programs, 57, 63
Volunteer plan, and teacher assignment, 151

W

Wagner, T., 96
Waivers, 50–51, 52
Warner-King, K., 51, 52, 146–148
Washington State, 131, 146–148
Wasley, P. A., 10
Wellness Program, 152
West Clermont Local School District, 8, 74–76, 99
West Clermont, Ohio, 99, 131, 145
Wichterle, S., 10
Wood, G., 94, 100–101
Work-based learning, 77
Workgroups, 47

Y

Year Two evaluation report, 43
YES (Youth Empowerment School), 66–67, 128–129
York, G., 72–73, 110, 114
Younger students, 125, 127, 130–131
Youth Congress, 65–66
Youth Empowerment School (YES), 66–67, 128–129
Youth Forums, 65–66

Z

"Zoo School," 5
Zucker, I., 86
Zuckerman, D., 50